The
Challenge of
CHANGE

SECOND EDITION

D0279922

Edited by
MICHAEL FULLAN

The
Challenge of
CHANGE

Start School Improvement Now!

SECOND EDITION

CORWIN
A SAGE Company

For information:

Corwin
A SAGE Company
2455 Teller Road
Thousand Oaks, California 91320
(800) 233-9936
Fax: (800) 417-2466
www.corwinpress.com

SAGE Ltd.
1 Oliver's Yard
55 City Road
London EC1Y 1SP
United Kingdom

SAGE India Pvt. Ltd.
B 1/I 1 Mohan Cooperative
Industrial Area
Mathura Road, New Delhi
India 110 044

SAGE Asia-Pacific Pte. Ltd.
33 Pekin Street #02-01
Far East Square
Singapore 048763

Printed in the United States of America.

A catalog record of this book is available from the Library of Congress.

ISBN 978-1-4129-5375-7 (cloth)
ISBN 978-1-4129-5376-4 (pbk.)

This book is printed on acid-free paper.

09   10   11   12   13   10   9   8   7   6   5   4   3   2   1

Acquisitions Editor:	Arnis Burvikovs
Associate Editor:	Desirée A. Bartlett
Production Editor:	Cassandra Margaret Seibel
Copy Editor:	Adam Dunham
Typesetter:	C&M Digitals (P) Ltd.
Proofreader:	Susan Schon
Indexer:	Jean Casalegno
Cover Designer:	Michael Dubowe

Contents

Acknowledgments

Grateful acknowledgment is made to the following authors and agents for their permission to reprint copyrighted materials.

Part One

The National Staff Development Council for "8 Forces for Leaders of Change" by Michael Fullan, Claudia Cuttress, and Ann Kilcher from the *Journal of Staff Development,* Volume 26, 2005, pp. 54–58. Reprinted with permission of the National Staff Development Council, www.nsdc.org, 2008. All rights reserved.

Harvard Education Publishing Group for "The Road to School Improvement" by Richard F. Elmore and Elizabeth A. City from *Harvard Education Letter,* Volume 23(3), May/June 2007, pp. 1–3. Copyright © by the President and Fellows of Harvard College. All rights reserved. For more information, please visit www.edletter.org or call 1-800-513-0763.

Association for Supervision and Curriculum Development for "The Fourth Way of Change" by Andy Hargreaves and Dennis Shirley from *Educational Leadership,* Volume 66(2), October 2008, pp. 56–61. Copyright © 2008 by ASCD. Used with permission. Learn more about ASCD at www.ascd.org.

Association for Supervision and Curriculum Development for "Transforming High Schools" by Pedro A. Noguera from *Educational Leadership,* Volume 61(8), May 2004, pp. 26–31. Copyright © 2004 by ASCD. Used with permission. Learn more about ASCD at www.ascd.org.

Part Two

Teachers College Press for "The Principal and Change" by Michael Fullan from *The New Meaning of Educational Change,* 4th edition (2007), Chapter 8, pp. 155–169. Copyright © 2007 by Teachers College, Columbia University. All rights reserved. Used with permission.

Corwin for "Breakthrough Components" by Michael Fullan, Peter Hill, and Carmel Crévola from *Breakthrough* (2006), Chapter 2, pp. 13–26. Copyright © by Corwin. Used with permission.

Solution Tree for "New Insights into Professional Learning Communities at Work" by Rick DuFour, Rebecca DuFour, and Bob Eaker from *Revisiting Professional Learning Communities at Work* (2006), Chapter 1, pp. 13–30. Copyright © by Solution Tree. Used with permission.

Corwin for "Coaches as Leaders of Change" by Jim Knight from *Instructional Coaching* (2007), Chapter 9, pp. 197–218. Copyright © by Corwin. Used with permission.

Paul Chapman for "Developing and Sustaining School Principals" by Kenneth Leithwood, Scott Bauer, and Brian Riedlinger from *Developing Sustainable Leadership* (2007), Chapter 20, pp. 97–115. Copyright © by Paul Chapman. Reprinted with permission of Sage Publications, Ltd.

Part Three

Paul Chapman for "Sustaining Leadership in Complex Times" by Michael Fullan and Lyn Sharratt from *Developing Sustainable Leadership* (2007), Chapter 20, pp. 116–136. Copyright © by Paul Chapman. Reprinted with permission of Sage Publications, Ltd.

Harvard Education Publishing for "The PELP Coherence Framework" by Stacey Childress, Richard F. Elmore, Allen Grossman, and Susan Moore Johnson from *Managing School Districts for High Performance* (2007), pp. 2–5. Copyright © by Harvard Education Publishing Group. All rights reserved. Used with permission.

Part Four

Sage Publications for "Learning About System Renewal" by Ben Levin and Michael Fullan from *Educational Management Administration & Leadership,* Volume 36, April 2008, pp. 289–303. Copyright © by Sage Publications All rights reserved. Used with permission.

Michael Barber for "Education, Equity, and the Economy" by Michael Barber. Adapted from a speech given at the National Education Summit, Washington, DC, September 15, 2008. Copyright © by Michael Barber. Used with permission.

About the Editor

 **Michael Fullan** is professor emeritus of the Ontario Institute for Studies in Education of the University of Toronto. Recognized as a worldwide authority on educational reform, he is engaged in training, consulting, and evaluating change projects around the world, and his books have been published in many languages.

Michael Fullan is currently Special Advisor to the Premier and Minister of Education in Ontario. His book, *Leading in a Culture of Change,* was awarded the 2002 Book of the Year Award by the National Staff Development Council, and *Breakthrough* (with Peter Hill and Carmel Crévola) won the 2006 Book of the Year Award from the American Association of Colleges for Teacher Education. His latest books are *The Six Secrets of Change* (Jossey-Bass), *What's Worth Fighting for in the Principalship* (Teachers College Press), and *Turnaround Leadership in Higher Education* (with Geoff Scott, Jossey-Bass).

A list of his widely acclaimed books, articles, and other resources can be found at www.michaelfullan.ca.

About the Contributors

Scott C. Bauer serves as associate professor in the Education Leadership program at George Mason University. His research interests involve the application of organizational design and theory to the improvement of schools and the efficacy of various strategies used to develop school leaders at all levels. His most recent publications deal with the development of teacher leaders, and he is involved in a three-year study of the implementation and effectiveness of a cross-district coaching and mentoring support system for new principals. He serves on the editorial boards of *Educational Administration Quarterly, Journal of School Leadership,* and *Journal of Research for Educational Leaders.*

Sir Michael Barber is a partner at McKinsey and Company, leading its global education practice. He has been working on major challenges of performance, organization, and reform in government and the public services, especially education, in the United States, United Kingdom, and other countries.

From 2001–2005, he was the founder and first Head of the Prime Minister's Delivery Unit where he was responsible for the oversight of implementation of British Prime Minister Tony Blair's priority programs including education. From 1997–2001, Michael was chief adviser to the U.K. Secretary of State for Education on School Standards, responsible for the implementation of the government's school reform program. Prior to joining government, Michael Barber was a professor at the Institute of Education, University of London. He is the author of *Instruction to Deliver: Fighting to Reform Britain's Public Services* (Methuen, 2008) and numerous other books and articles.

Stacey Childress is a lecturer in the General Management unit at Harvard Business School and a cofounder of the Public Education

Leadership Project at Harvard University. Stacey studies entrepreneurial activity in public education in the United States. She has authored more than two dozen case studies about large urban districts and entrepreneurial education ventures and is the coauthor of the Harvard Business Review article, "How to Manage Urban Districts." Stacey teaches in Harvard Business School's (HBS) MBA program. In 2008, she was an inaugural recipient of the Charles M. Williams Award for excellence in teaching, named in honor of one of the School's most celebrated case method teachers. She also teaches in executive education programs at HBS and around Harvard.

Elizabeth A. City helps educators improve learning and teaching through leadership development and the strategic use of data and resources. She is director of instructional strategy at the Executive Leadership Program for Educators at Harvard University. Her publications include: *Resourceful Leadership: Tradeoffs and Tough Decisions on the Road to School Improvement* (Cambridge, MA: Harvard Education Press, 2008); *The Teacher's Guide to Leading Student-Centered Discussions: Talking About Texts in the Classroom* (Thousand Oaks, CA: Corwin, 2006); and *Data Wise: A Step-by-Step Guide to Using Assessment Results to Improve Teaching and Learning* (Cambridge, MA: Harvard Education Press, 2005).

Carmel Crévola is an independent educational consultant. Her primary areas of expertise are in the fields of literacy teaching and learning, assessment, school effectiveness and improvement, tri-level reform processes, and her current area of research focuses on the role of oral language in literacy acquisition and student success. She is currently involved in school reform projects in Canada, England, the United States, and Peru. She has a new book due to be published in 2009 by Nelson Publishing and Corwin titled *Speak Up: Breakthrough Oral Language Instruction K–6*.

Claudia Cuttress is development manager at Michael Fullan Enterprises. You can reach her by e-mail: ccuttress@oise.utoronto.ca.

Rebecca DuFour has been a teacher, administrator, and central office coordinator. Under her guidance as principal, her school became a model professional learning community. She has coauthored seven books about developing professional learning communities and has written for journals and other publications. She continues to present and write about professional learning communities.

Richard DuFour spent 34 years as a public school teacher, principal, or superintendent. From 1983 to 1991, he was principal of Adlai Stevenson High School in Illinois and then served as that district's superintendent from 1991 through 2002. Throughout his tenure, he raised the achievement bar, making Adlai Stevenson High School recognized throughout the nation as an example of best educational practices. He presents and writes extensively on the development of professional learning communities.

Robert Eaker is a professor in the Department of Educational Leadership at Middle Tennessee State University, where he also served as dean of the College of Education and interim vice president and provost. He is a former fellow with the National Center for Effective Schools Research and Development and has written about effective teaching, effective schools, helping teachers use research findings, and high expectations for student achievement. He continues to write and present on developing professional learning communities, raising expectations, and learning.

Richard F. Elmore's research focuses on the effects of federal, state, and local education policy on schools and classrooms. He is currently exploring how schools of different types and in different policy contexts develop a sense of accountability and a capacity to deliver high-quality instruction. He has also researched educational choice, school restructuring, and how changes in teaching and learning affect school organization. Elmore is director of the Consortium for Policy Research in Education (CPRE), a group of universities engaged in research on state and local education policy, funded by the U.S. Department of Education. He teaches regularly in programs for public-sector executives. Elmore has held positions with the Department of Health, Education, and Welfare and the U.S. Office of Education (1969–1971), as well as several government advisory positions at the city, state, and national levels.

Allen Grossman was appointed a Harvard Business School Professor of Management Practice in July 2000. He joined the Business School faculty in July 1998, with a concurrent appointment as a visiting scholar at the Harvard Graduate School of Education. He served as president and chief executive officer of Outward Bound USA for six years before stepping down in 1997 to work on the challenges of creating high-performing nonprofit organizations. His current research focuses on leading and governing high-performing nonprofit organizations and leadership and management of public school districts.

Andy Hargreaves is the Thomas More Brennan Chair in Education at Boston College. He has written or edited almost 30 books, including *Teaching in the Knowledge Society* (2003), which received Outstanding Book prizes from the American Educational Research Association and the American Libraries Association; *Sustainable Leadership* (2006) with Dean Fink; *Change Wars* (2008) with Michael Fullan; and *The Fourth Way* (2009) with Dennis Shirley.

Peter Hill retired as secretary general of the Hong Kong Examinations and Assessment Authority (HKEAA) on Friday, December 14, 2007. He has held numerous senior positions in school administration and educational research in Australia and the United States, including as head of the school system in the State of Victoria, Australia, and as professor of leadership and management in the Faculty of Education of the University of Melbourne. More recently, he was director of research and development at the National Center on Education and the Economy in the United States. Over the past decade, he has directed and assisted in a number of large-scale, comprehensive school-improvement projects. His research interests are in the fields of assessment, school effectiveness and improvement, and instructional leadership.

Susan Moore Johnson is a professor at the Harvard Graduate School of Education, where she directs the Project on the Next Generation of Teachers. She codirects the Public Education Leadership Project. She is the lead author of *Finders and Keepers: Helping New Teachers Survive and Thrive in Our Schools* (2004) and *Leading the Local* (2007), a study of local teachers union presidents.

Ann Kilcher is an independent consultant and president of the Paideia Consulting Group. You can contact her at 6020 Binney St., Halifax, Nova Scotia, Canada B3H 2C1, (902) 429-3282, fax (902) 492-2144, e-mail: akilcher@pefchattanooga.org.

Jim Knight is the director of the Kansas Coaching Project (www.instructionalcoach.org) at the University of Kansas Center for Research on Learning. He has written several books and articles about instructional coaching, including *Instructional Coaching: A Partnership Approach to Improving Instruction.*

Kenneth Leithwood is professor of educational leadership and policy at OISE, University of Toronto. His most recent books include *Distributed Leadership According to the Evidence* (Routledge, 2008) and *Leading With Teachers' Emotions in Mind* (Corwin, 2008). Professor Leithwood is the recent recipient of the University of Toronto's Impact on Public Policy award and a Fellow of the Royal Society of Canada.

Ben Levin is Canada Research Chair in education policy and leadership at OISE, University of Toronto. His career includes senior roles in governments as well as an academic and research career. His latest book is *How to Change 5000 Schools* (Harvard Education Press, 2008).

Pedro A. Noguera is a professor in the Steinhardt School of Education at New York University and the director of the Metropolitan Center for Urban Education. An urban sociologist, Noguera's scholarship and research focuses on the ways in which schools are influenced by social and economic conditions in the urban environment. From 2000 to 2003, Noguera served as the Judith K. Dimon Professor of Communities and Schools at the Harvard Graduate School of Education. From 1990 to 2000, he was a professor in social and cultural studies at the Graduate School of Education and the director of the Institute for the Study of Social Change at the University of California, Berkeley. Pedro Noguera has published over one hundred and fifty research articles, monographs, and research reports on topics such as urban school reform, conditions that promote student achievement, youth violence, the potential impact of school choice and vouchers on urban public schools, and race and ethnic relations in American society.

Brian Riedlinger has served as CEO of the Algiers Charter School Association (ACSA) since November of 2005. As CEO, he opened six schools on the West Bank of New Orleans, educating about 3800 students in 2005 and 2006, the first group of schools to open after Katrina. ACSA has opened three more schools for a total of nine, currently educating nearly 5000 students. In addition, Brian Riedlinger serves as CEO of the School Leadership Center of Greater New Orleans—a "principals' center" dedicated to the improvement of school leadership and, therefore, student achievement, through professional development of school leaders. Previously, he was a principal in the New Orleans Public Schools for 20 years and was selected State Principal of the Year in 1999. Brian received his bachelor's and master's degrees from Louisiana State University and his doctorate from the University of New Orleans.

Lyn Sharratt is senior advisor, System and School Improvement, in York Region District School Board, Ontario, Canada. Prior to this, Lyn was superintendent of Curriculum and Instructional Services in York Region. She has written many educational journal articles and presented internationally on district reform. Lyn is an Associate at OISE, University of Toronto, where she received her doctorate in 1996.

Dennis Shirley is professor of education at the Lynch School of Education at Boston College. He is a leading-edge scholar in the area of community organizing and educational change and is recipient of a past awards and fellowships from the Alexander von Humboldt Foundation in Bonn, Germany, and the Rockefeller Study and Conference Center in Bellagio, Italy.

PART I

Change Forces

Michael Fullan

There are large changes at work affecting all levels of the system. The four articles in this section provide a range of perspectives on the main issues.

In a project for Microsoft, Fullan, Cuttress, and Kilcher (2005) developed an "elite course" on leading change in which they identified eight major change forces that all leaders would have to understand, contend with, and address in order to survive and thrive in addressing the complex change challenges into the 21st century.

Elmore and City take us on the "road to school improvement." Elmore, one of the most incisive analysts and actors in large-scale reform, concludes that this road is "hard, bumpy, and takes as long as it takes," and offers ideas for surviving the bumps and going to the next level.

Hargreaves and Shirley propose a "Fourth Way" to reform, which in effect is "building from the bottom" and steering from the top.

Noguera takes us into the murky world of "transforming urban high schools" and paints a dim picture of the challenges facing secondary schools and then turns his attention to identifying promising pathways to success.

As a set, the four articles in Part One furnish a valuable context for the other three parts, each of which delves into each of the levels of tri-level reform.

CHAPTER ONE

Introduction to The Challenge of Change

Purposeful Action at Work

Michael Fullan

The first edition of *The Challenge of Change* was published in 1997. It turned out that this was precisely the year when the field of educational change began a major shift toward deeper action and large-scale reform.

The occasion was Tony Blair's first term election in England in May, 1997. He came into office with a clear and explicit education platform in which literacy and numeracy were named as the core priorities. Blair and his government committed in advance to targets of 80% proficiency in literacy and 75% in numeracy for 11-year-olds—starting at a base of 62%. This was an enormous undertaking because it involved the entire system of 20,000 schools and a timeline of essentially four years.

What was more significant was that Blair and his team, led by chief architect of strategy, Michael Barber, said that they would base their strategy on existing *change knowledge*. By that they meant that they would combine "pressure and support"—the *pressure* of targets, monitoring progress, feeding back data, and intervening in cases of low performance; *support* meant investing in "capacity building" through establishing new positions at the school, district, and

3

government levels to lead literacy and numeracy through intensive professional learning opportunities focusing on instructional improvement and through the development and spread of new high quality curriculum materials.

The good news was that the strategy worked—to a point. Proficiency scores increased from 62% to 75% in literacy and from 62% to 73% in numeracy by 2002 (in fact by 2000). For the first time, we were able to prove to politicians that significant results could be obtained on a large scale "within one election period"—still not reaching the high aspiration targets, but impressive indeed.

The bad news was that the results plateaued from 2000 onward. In our evaluation of the initiative, we attributed this to two things. One was that the strategy was too driven from the top and as such did not get deep enough into the hearts and minds of teachers and principals. The second and related reason was that the government failed to adjust the strategy and in fact did not keep the priority at a high enough level as it entered a second term in 2001.

My point is that the effort in England was a kind of coming out of change knowledge from the domain of research to the domain of action. Much of this knowledge incidentally has been chronicled and captured in the fourth edition of *The New Meaning of Educational Change* (Fullan, 2007).

TRI-LEVEL REFORM

We have come to call this approach to system change *tri-level reform* (see Figure 1.1).

In order to bring about sustained reform in any school, we need to move beyond treating one school at a time to addressing all schools simultaneously. To do so means that the district must have its act together (a system of schools, if you like) and that the state (or in the case of federal systems, state and federal) must also approach change from a tri-level perspective.

Many of the articles in this collection (which I will turn to shortly) get at the details of tri-level reform, but at this point I will provide an overview. Tri-level reform does not mean that you wait for the other two levels to get their act together. Whatever level you are operating from requires two things: a focus on your own internal development (a school, a district, or whatever), while at the same time seeking connections with other levels. My own view, not always

Figure 1.1   Tri-Level Reform

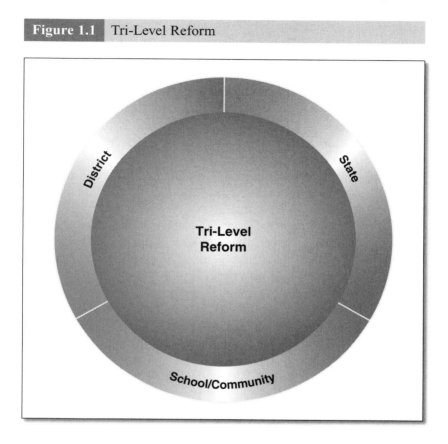

obtainable, is to establish a system of not only greater alignment across the three levels but, even more important, greater *permeable connectivity,* that is, more two-way interaction, communication, and mutual influence.

This is not just theory. We have, in fact, been putting this set of ideas into place in Ontario since 2003, when the liberal government came into power (Fullan, 2008a). I have had the privilege of serving as the Premier's education advisor as we have, and still are, establishing a systematic set of policies and strategies to transform the system in Ontario—a large scale proposition involving two million students, 4,000 elementary schools, and 900 secondary schools across 72 school districts.

We have focused on three core priorities (we recommend that large systems focus on a small number of ambitious goals as core, do these well, and stay the course). Our goals focus on high proficiency in literacy and numeracy (i.e., including higher-order thinking and problem solving) and high school graduation. In terms of numbers, these rates of achieving in Ontario were stagnant for the five years prior to the new set of strategies implemented in 2003. Literacy and numeracy rates hovered around 54% proficiency (remember we are using high cut-off points here) and 69% high school graduation. As of 2008, literacy and numeracy have improved to 65% and high school graduation has improved to 75%—still not full success but strong and continuing progress.

Details of the Ontario strategy are contained in Chapter 13 of this book, but I can provide here the basic assumptions and components of the strategy (see Figure 1.2).

The six components in Figure 1.2 work together. Direction and sector engagement involves direction from the top combined with

Figure 1.2   A Theory of Action for System Reform

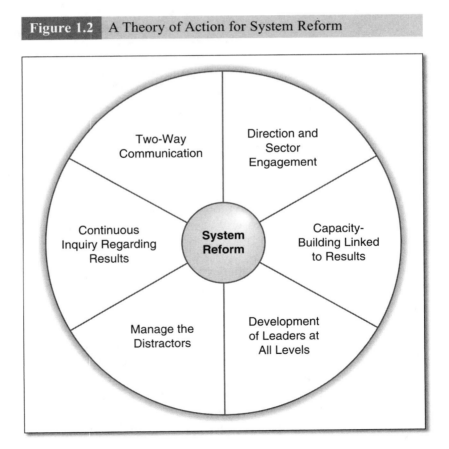

partnership with the field (schools and districts). It is explicitly presented as neither top-down nor bottom-up, but rather as a *blended* strategy. It involves an inspirational overall vision, a small number of ambitious goals publicly stated (in this case, literacy, numeracy, and high school graduation), a guiding coalition (a leadership team at the top who works together), investment of resources, and a sense of flexibility with the field (schools and districts).

Second, instead of leading with accountability, capacity building is at the heart of the strategy. This component consists of strategies and actions that mobilize *capacity,* defined as new knowledge, skills, and competencies. For example, a focus on effective instructional practices in literacy and numeracy, combined with the development and support of coaches, mentors, and new instructional leadership roles for principals, enables the system to identify and implement new capacities linked to results, namely, greater student achievement. There is continuous attention paid to data on students results—are we making progress, is the progress affecting all subgroups, when do we need to intervene at specific schools and districts to improve capacity in order to get better results, and so on.

Third, and related, all of this work requires a strong infrastructure to support and propel it. This occurs at all three levels—school leaders, district staff, and state or province department staff.

Fourth, and equally important, is a commitment to manage the distractions. In complex political systems, distractions are ubiquitous and inevitable. We make a conscious effort to focus on the small number of goals, to stay the course, to minimize ad hoc initiatives, and to make time available for instructional development.

Fifth, because there are things to learn during implementation, we engage in continuous evaluation and inquiry—what are effective practices, what can we learn from specific examples of school and district success, and how can we spread the word across the system.

Finally, there is continuous two-way communication between the government and the schools and districts. This serves simultaneously to communicate the vision, to detect and respond to problems, and to mark and celebrate success.

MORAL PURPOSE AND INSTRUCTIONAL REFORM

As part and parcel of the new developments since 1997, in addressing the whole system there has also been a move to go deeper into moral purpose and instructional improvements. *Moral purpose* consists of the abiding commitment to raise the bar and close the gap for *all* students, regardless of background. Moral purpose by itself is just rhetoric, so this is why the actual strategies of change are so crucial. These strategies must be in the service of fulfilling moral purpose. This goal has been enabled by new developments in pedagogical practice. In literacy, numeracy, and other realms of teaching and learning, there has been an overall impressive development in identifying high-yield instructional practices.

Education, compared to many other professions, has been slow to focus on "the black box of instruction" in order to develop, identify, and spread specific, high-yield practices that are known to get results (Fullan, Hill, & Crévola, 2006). Several of the chapters in this collection delve into these trends.

In sum, the big shift since 1997 has been an explicit focus on action—action that addresses the whole system, action that has both greater moral purpose and the means of fulfilling it. Moreover, we are seeing that the fundamental ideas embedded in these strategies have a sound basis in practice across all sectors—business and public entities alike (Fullan, 2008b).

What these developments have done is not so much solved the problem but basically opened the door to considering more radical reform. I expect that in the next decade we will see more purposeful experiments in attempts to go wider as well as deeper.

In the meantime, this collection helps to pave the way. I provide more specific brief introductions to each of the remaining three sections. The "challenge of change" is everyone's favorite phrase these days. And for good reason. Never in education has the need been greater for reform that results in both individual and societal benefits.

REFERENCES

Fullan, M. (2007). *The new meaning of educational change.* New York: Teachers College Press.

Fullan, M. (2008a). Have theory will travel: A theory of action for system change. In A. Hargreaves & M. Fullan (Eds.), *Change wars* (pp. 274–293). Bloomington, IN: Solution Tree.

Fullan, M. (2008b). *The six secrets of change.* San Francisco: Jossey-Bass.

Fullan, M., Cuttress, C., & Kilcher, A. (2005). 8 forces for leaders of change. *Journal of Staff Development, 26*(4), 8–13.

Fullan, M., Hill, P., & Crévola, C. (2006). *Breakthrough.* Thousand Oaks, CA: Corwin; Toronto: Ontario Principals' Council.

CHAPTER TWO

8 Forces for Leaders of Change

Michael Fullan

Claudia Cuttress

Ann Kilcher

Presence of the core concepts does not guarantee success,
but their absence ensures failure.

The history of educational reform and innovation is replete with good ideas or policies that fail to get implemented or that are successful in one situation but not in another. A missing ingredient in most failed cases is appreciation and use of what we call *change knowledge:* understanding and insight about the process of change and the key drivers that make for successful change in practice. The presence of change knowledge does not guarantee success, but its absence ensures failure.

It is not easy to rectify this deficit. Policymakers do not want to be slowed down by knowledge of change. It takes time to address

Author's Note: Work in developing ideas for leading change has been funded through the Partners in Learning Initiative, Microsoft.

this knowledge—even though, ironically, they are eventually slowed down even more by failed implementation.

In the past 20 years, we have learned a great deal about innovative processes that work and those that don't. We are using this knowledge to bring about system change across the three levels of school and community, district, and state (Barber & Fullan, 2005). In particular, eight drivers are keys to create effective and lasting change.

1. ENGAGING PEOPLE'S MORAL PURPOSES

The first overriding principle is knowledge about the why of change, namely *moral purpose.* Moral purpose in educational change is about improving society through improving educational systems and thus the learning of all citizens.

In education, moral purpose involves committing to raise the bar and close the gap in student achievement—for example, increasing literacy for all, with special attention to those most disadvantaged. There is a wide gap, particularly in some countries, between groups at the bottom and those at the top. Schools need to "raise the floor" by figuring out how to speed up the learning of those who are at the bottom, those for whom the school system has been less effective.

Improving overall literacy achievement is directly associated with a country's economic productivity. In countries where the gap between high and low student performance is reduced, citizens' health and well-being are measurably better.

In change knowledge, moral purpose is not just a goal but also a process of engaging educators, community leaders, and society as a whole in the moral purpose of reform. If moral purpose is front and center, the remaining seven drivers become additional forces for enacting moral purpose.

2. BUILDING CAPACITY

The second driver is *building capacity,* which involves policies, strategies, resources, and actions designed to increase people's collective power to move the system forward (schools, districts, states). Building capacity involves developing new knowledge, skills, and competencies; new resources (time, ideas, materials); and new shared identity and motivation to work together for greater change.

In addition to individual and collective capacity as defined by increased knowledge, resources, and motivation, organizational capacity involves improving infrastructure. The infrastructure consists of agencies at the local, regional, and state levels that can deliver new capacity in the system, such as training, consulting, and other support.

Capacity often is the missing element, even when people agree on the need for change. For example, to improve literacy, teachers and principals must develop new skills and increased commitment in the face of inevitable obstacles (see the third driver). Similarly, in the case of new technologies, not only must educators acquire new skills and understandings, they must also integrate these technologies into curriculum, teaching, learning, and assessing learning.

Capacity building is a collective phenomenon. Whole schools, whole districts, and whole systems must increase their capacity as groups. Building group capacity is difficult because it involves working together in new ways.

Capacity must be evident in practice and be ongoing. Front-end training is insufficient. It does not translate into improvements in the daily cultures of how people need to work in new ways.

3. UNDERSTANDING THE CHANGE PROCESS

Understanding the *change process* is a big driver because such understanding cuts across all elements. The process of change is also difficult and frustrating to grasp because it requires leaders to take into account factors that they would rather not have to stop and deal with. They would rather lay out the purpose and plan and get on with it. Change doesn't work that way.

Making change work requires the energy, ideas, commitment, and ownership of all those who are implementing improvements. The urgency of many problems, however, does not allow for long-term "ownership development." (In fact, more leisurely strategies do not produce greater ownership anyway.)

Ownership is not something available at the beginning of a change process but something created through a quality change process. Put differently, shared vision and ownership are more the outcome of a quality change process than they are a precondition.

The change process is about establishing the condition for continuous improvement in order to persist and overcome inevitable barriers to reform. It is about innovativeness, not just innovation.

4. Developing Cultures for Learning

The fourth driver, *cultures for learning,* sounds general but means something specific in establishing the conditions for success. Developing a culture for learning involves a set of strategies designed for people to learn from each other (the knowledge dimension) and become collectively committed to improvement (the affective dimension).

Successful change involves learning during implementation. One of the most powerful drivers of change involves learning from peers, especially those who are further along in implementing new ideas. We can think of such learning inside the school and local community and across schools or jurisdictions. Within the school, there is a great deal of practical research that demonstrates the necessity and power of professional learning communities (Dufour, Eaker, & Dufour, 2005).

Fred Newmann and his colleagues (Newmann, King, & Youngs, 2000) identified five components of change capacity within the school, including developing new knowledge and skills, establishing professional learning communities, building program coherence, accessing new resources, and developing principal/school leadership. Schools and their communities must develop new cultures of learning in order to improve.

When school systems establish cultures of learning, they constantly seek and develop teachers' knowledge and skills required to create effective new learning experiences for students. In addition to school and community learning, a powerful new strategy is evolving which we call "lateral capacity building," involving strategies in which schools and communities learn from each other within a given district or region and beyond. Learning from others widens the pool of ideas and also enhances a greater "we-we" identity beyond one school (Fullan, 2005).

Knowledge sharing and collective identity are powerful forces for positive change, and they form a core component of our change knowledge. We need to value these aspects and know how to put them into action. Jeffrey Pfeffer and Robert Sutton (2000) reinforce this conclusion in their analysis of *The Knowing-Doing Gap.* They claim that we should embed more of the process of acquiring new knowledge in the actual doing of the task and less in formal training programs that are frequently ineffective (p. 27). Change knowledge has a bias for action. Developing a climate where people learn from each other within and across units, and being preoccupied with turning good knowledge into action, is essential. Turning information into actionable knowledge is a social process. Thus, developing learning cultures is crucial. Good policies and ideas take off in learning cultures, but they go nowhere in cultures of isolation.

5. DEVELOPING CULTURES OF EVALUATION

A *culture of evaluation* must be coupled with a culture of learning for schools to sort out promising from not-so-promising ideas and especially to deepen the meaning of what is learned. One of the highest-yield strategies for educational change recently developed is assessment *for* learning (not just assessment *of* learning). Assessment for learning incorporates

- accessing/gathering data on student learning,
- disaggregating data for more detailed understanding,
- developing action plans based on the previous two points in order to make improvements, and
- being able to articulate and discuss performance with parents and external groups.

When schools and school systems increase their collective capacity to engage in ongoing assessment for learning, they achieve major improvements. Several other aspects of evaluation cultures are important, including school-based self-appraisal, meaningful use of external accountability data, and what Jim Collins (2001) found in "great" organizations, namely a commitment to "confronting the brutal facts" and establishing a culture of disciplined inquiry.

Cultures of evaluation serve external accountability as well as internal data processing purposes. They produce data on an ongoing basis that enables groups to use information for action planning as well as for external accounting (see Black, Harrison, Lee, Marshall, & Wiliam, 2003; Stiggins, 2001).

One other matter: Technology has become an enormously necessary and powerful tool in our work on assessment, as it makes it possible to access and analyze student achievement data on an ongoing basis, take corrective action, and share best solutions. Developing cultures of evaluation and capacity to use technology for improvement must go hand-in-hand; both are seriously underdeveloped in most systems.

6. FOCUSING ON LEADERSHIP FOR CHANGE

One of the most powerful lessons for change involves *leadership*. Here, change knowledge consists of knowing what kind of leadership is best for leading productive change. High-flying, charismatic leaders look like powerful change agents but are actually bad for business because too much revolves around the individuals themselves.

Leadership, to be effective, must spread throughout the organization. Collins (2001) found that charismatic leaders were negatively associated with sustainability. Leaders of the so-called "great" organizations were characterized by "deep personal humility" and "intense professional will" (p. 22). Collins talks about the importance of leadership that "builds enduring greatness" in the organization rather than focusing on short-term results.

The main mark of a school principal at the end of his or her tenure is not just that individual's impact on student achievement but rather how many leaders are left behind who can go even further. Henry Mintzberg (2004) makes the same point: "Successful managing is not about one's own success but about fostering success in others" (p. 16). And, "While managers have to make decisions, far more important, especially in large networked organizations of knowledge works, is what they do to enhance decision-making capabilities of others" (p. 38).

Change knowledge, then, means seeking leaders who represent innovativeness—the capacity to develop leadership in others on an ongoing basis. We need to produce a critical mass of leaders who have change knowledge. Such leaders produce and feed on other leadership through the system. There is no other driver as essential as leadership for sustainable reform.

7. FOSTERING COHERENCE MAKING

When innovation runs amok, even if driven by moral purpose, the result is overload and fragmentation. To a certain extent, this is normal in complex systems.

Change knowledge is required to render overload into greater coherence. Creating coherence is a never-ending proposition that involves alignment, connecting the dots, and being clear about how the big picture fits together. Above all, *coherence making* involves investing in capacity building so that cultures of learning and evaluation, through the proliferation of leadership, can create their own coherence on the ground.

Change knowledge is not about developing the greatest number of innovations but rather about achieving new patterns of coherence that enable people to focus more deeply on how strategies for effective learning interconnect.

8. Cultivating Tri-Level Development

The eighth and final driver lies in the realization that we are talking about system transformation at three levels. We are not talking just about changing individuals, but also about changing systems—what we call the *tri-level model.*

Here is a tri-level lens on a problem:

- What has to happen at the school and community level?
- What has to happen at the district level?
- What has to happen at the state level?

We need to change individuals, but we also need to change contexts. We need to develop better individuals while we simultaneously develop better organizations and systems. Such work is easier said than done and involves what we have recently called developing "system thinkers in action" (Fullan, 2005).

For our purposes, we need only say, "beware of the individualistic bias" where the tacit assumption is that if we change enough individuals, then the system will change. In such cases, change won't happen. We need to change systems at the same time. To change individuals and systems simultaneously, we must provide more "learning in context"—that is, learning in the actual situations we want to change. Mintzberg (2004) focuses on this when he says,

> Leadership is as much about doing in order to think as thinking in order to do. (p. 10)

> We need programs designed to educate practicing managers in context. (p. 193)

> Leadership has to be learned . . . not just by doing it, but by being able to gain conceptual insight while doing it. (p. 200)

In any case, tri-level development involves focusing on all three levels of the system and their interrelationships and giving people wider learning opportunities within these contexts as a route to changing the very contexts within which people work.

THE IMPORTANCE OF CHANGE KNOWLEDGE

Enough research on implementation has been done in the past 35 years for us to say that if you don't know the eight guiding principles/drivers of change (in the sense of being able to use them for insight and action), even the best ideas will not take hold. Without change knowledge, you get failure.

To achieve the goal, we must develop leaders who have greater change knowledge and who can, in turn, develop leadership in others. These developments do not involve just identifying and memorizing the knowledge base. Knowing is insufficient; only knowing-by-doing, reflecting, and redoing will move us forward.

Once people grasp the nature of change knowledge and appreciate its centrality to success, we have a chance of developing it further in practice. We must go beyond superficial knowledge of the key concepts and move toward a deeper commitment to developing knowledge, skills, and beliefs related to being change agents in collaboration with others.

When leaders and other participants have opportunities to learn more deeply in context, they have a chance of transforming the contexts that constrain them.

Power Principles

To push as hard as the process will allow while increasing the chances for success, understand that

Strategizing will help us evolve and reshape ideas and actions.

Change agents often are tempted to develop a complete strategic plan and then allocate mechanisms of accountability and support to implement it. The first lesson in the change process: The strategic plan is an innovation; it is not innovativeness.

We need strategy and strategic ideas, but above all, we need to think of the evolution of change plans as a process of shaping and reshaping ideas and actions. Henry Mintzberg, in his 2004 critique of existing MBA programs, captures this idea precisely:

> Strategy is an interactive process, not a two-step sequence; it requires continual feedback between thought and action. . . . Strategists have to be in touch; they have to know what they are strategizing about; they have to respond and react and adjust, often allowing strategies to *emerge*, step-by-step. In a word, they have to *learn*. (p. 55)

Effective change is more about strategizing, which is a process, than it is about strategy. The more that leaders practice strategizing, the more they hone their scientific and intuitive knowledge of change.

Pressure means ambitious targets.
Support involves developing new competencies.

The second element of understanding change dynamics is realizing that large-scale reform requires combining and integrating pressure and support.

Social systems include a great deal of inertia, which means they require new forces to change their direction. These new forces involve the judicious use of pressure and support.

Pressure means ambitious targets, transparent evaluation and monitoring, calling upon moral purpose, and the like. *Support* involves developing new competencies, access to new ideas, more time for learning, and collaboration.

The more that pressure and support become seamless, the more effective the change process will be at getting things to happen. As the eight drivers of change operate in concert, pressure and support, in effect, start to get built in to the ongoing culture of interaction.

Knowledge of the implementation dip can reduce
the awkwardness of the learning period.

The third aspect of understanding the change process is to understand the finding that all eventual successful change proceeds through an implementation dip (Fullan, 2001).

(Continued)

(Continued)

Since change involves grappling with new beliefs and understandings, and new skills, competencies, and behaviors, changes will not go smoothly in the early stages of implementation (even if there has been implementation preparation). This applies to any individual, but is much more complex when many people simultaneously are involved.

Knowing about the implementation dip helps in working with change initiatives. First, it has brought out into the open the fact that all changes worth their salt involve a somewhat awkward learning period. Second, such knowledge has resulted in us being able to reduce the period of awkwardness. By being aware of the problem, we are able to use strategies (support, training, etc.) that reduce the implementation dip from (in the case of school change) three years to half that time. This obviously depends on the starting conditions and complexity of the change, but the point is that without knowledge of the implementation dip, problems persist and people give up without giving the idea a chance.

Shorter implementation dips are more tolerable, and once gains start to be made earlier, motivation increases. Note that motivation is increasing (or not) during the implementation process. This is a sign of a quality (or poor) change process.

The next two elements of understanding the change process—the fear of change and technical versus adaptive challenges—delve deeper into the implementation dip.

Mastering implementation is necessary to overcome the fear of change.

The fear of change is classical change knowledge. People need to know that at the beginning of the change process, the losses are specific and tangible (it is clear what is being left behind), but gains are theoretical and distant. This is so by definition. One cannot realize the gains without mastering implementation, and this takes time. In addition, those making changes don't necessarily have confidence that the gains will be attained. It is a theoretical proposition.

Stewart Black and Hal Gregersen (2002) talk about "brain barriers," such as the failure to move in new directions even when the direction is clear. The clearer the new vision, the more immobilized people become. Why? Their answer:

The clearer the new vision, the easier it is for people to see all the specific ways in which they will be incompetent and look stupid.

Many prefer to be competent at the [old] wrong thing than incompetent at the [new] right thing. (p. 70)

In other words, an additional element of change process knowledge involves realizing that clear, even inspiring, visions are insufficient. People need the right combinations of pressure and support to become adept and comfortable with "the new right way."

It is necessary to identify the distinction between technical problems and adaptive challenges.

The fifth element comes from Ron Heifetz and Marty Linsky's (2002) distinction between technical problems and adaptive challenges.

Technical problems are those in which current knowledge is sufficient to address the problem. Technical problems are still difficult, and people will experience the usual implementation dip, but they are solvable in terms of what we know. Adaptive challenges are more complex, and the solutions go beyond what we know. Heifetz and Linsky identify these properties of adaptive challenges:

- Adaptive challenges demand a response beyond our current repertoire.
- Adaptive work to narrow the gap between our aspirations and current reality requires difficult learning.
- The people with the problem are the problem—and the solution.
- Adaptive work generates disequilibrium and avoidance.
- Adaptive work takes time.

Most of the big moral purpose goals we aspire to these days tend to be adaptive challenges. Change knowledge, then, involves strategizing with Heifetz's five assumptions in mind to set up a more realistic change process.

Engaging others in change requires persistence to overcome the inevitable challenges.

The final aspect of understanding change as a process is a kind of retrospective overlay of the previous five components.

Engaging others in the process of change requires persistence in order to overcome the inevitable challenges—to keep going despite setbacks—but it also involves adaptation and problem solving through being flexible enough to incorporate new ideas into strategizing.

Both focus and flexibility are needed.

(Continued)

(Continued)

The concept that captures persistence and flexibility is *resilience*. Because change is complex, difficult, and frustrating, the change process requires pushing ahead without being rigid, regrouping despite setbacks, and not being discouraged when progress is slow.

Persistence and resilience are important because people often start with grand intentions and aspirations, but gradually lower them over time in the face of obstacles. In the end, then, they achieve very little. Armed with change knowledge, education leaders should approach the change process with a commitment to maintain or even increase high standards and aspirations. Obstacles should be seen as problems to be resolved to achieve high targets rather than reasons for consciously or unconsciously lowering aspirations.

REFERENCES

Barber, M., & Fullan, M. (2005, March 2). Tri-Level development: Putting systems thinking into action. *Education Week, 24*(25), 32–35.

Black, S., & Gregersen, H. (2002). *Leading strategic change: Breaking through the brain barrier.* New York: Prentice Hall.

Black, P., Harrison, C., Lee, C., Marshall, B., & Wiliam, D. (2003). *Assessment for learning.* Philadelphia: Open University Press.

Collins, J. (2001). *Good to great.* New York: HarperCollins.

Dufour, R., Eaker, R., & Dufour, R. (Eds.). (2005). *On common ground.* Bloomington, IN: National Education Service.

Fullan, M. (2001). *The new meaning of educational change* (3rd ed.). New York: Teachers College Press.

Fullan, M. (2005). *Leadership & sustainability: Systems thinkers in action.* Thousand Oaks, CA: Corwin.

Fullan, M., Cuttress, C., & Kilcher, A., (2005). 8 forces for change leaders. *Journal of Staff Development, 26*(4), 8–13.

Heifetz, R., & Linsky, M. (2002). *Leadership on the line: Staying alive through the dangers of leading.* Boston: Harvard Business School Press.

Mintzberg, H. (2004). *Managers not MBAs.* San Francisco: Berrett-Koehler.

Newmann, F., King, B., & Youngs, P. (2000). *Professional development that addresses school capacity.* Paper presented at the annual meeting of the American Educational Research Association.

Pfeffer, J., & Sutton, R. (2000). *The knowing-doing gap.* Boston: Harvard Business School Press.

Stiggins, R. (2001). *Student-involved classroom assessment* (3rd ed.). Columbus, OH: Merrill Prentice Hall.

CHAPTER THREE

The Road to School Improvement

Richard F. Elmore

Elizabeth A. City

It's hard, it's bumpy, and it takes as long as it takes.

I n our work on instructional improvement with low-performing schools, we are often asked, "How long does it take?" The next most frequently asked question is, "We're stuck. What should we do next?" In our roles as facilitators of communities of practice focused on instructional improvement, in our work on internal accountability (Richard) and using data (Liz), and in our research, we have noticed some distinct patterns in the way schools develop as they become more successful at improving student learning and measured performance. Here are a few of our observations.

There are no "breakthroughs" or dramatic "turnarounds" in the improvement of low-performing schools. There are, however, predictable periods of significant improvement, followed by periods of relative stasis or decline, followed again by periods of improvement.

Authors' Note: This chapter originally appeared in the May/June 2007 issue of the *Harvard Education Letter*.

This pattern of "punctuated equilibrium" is common across all types of human development: individual, organizational, economic, and sociopolitical.

A very low-performing school may see significant improvements in students' scores in the early stages of concerted work to improve instruction. These early periods of growth are almost always the result of making more efficient use of *existing resources*—instructional time, teachers' knowledge and skill, and leadership focus. For example, a school might extend time spent on math from 45 minutes a day to 60 minutes or might make smaller groups for literacy instruction. Not surprisingly, the improvements in performance that occur as a result of improvements in existing resources are relatively short term. They are usually followed by a period of flattened performance.

If a school is on a significant improvement trajectory, this plateau usually represents a process of incorporating new knowledge into the previous base of knowledge and skill. The school that extended time spent on math might now focus on what the math instruction looks like—how to teach mathematics so that students have a conceptual understanding of the math rather than only a procedural understanding. These changes are, by their very nature, extremely challenging. They challenge teachers' and administrators' existing ideas about what it is possible to do. They raise difficult questions about the effectiveness of past practices. They require unprecedented investments of time and energy. And often they do not produce immediate payoffs in measured student performance.

In our experience, most of the learning that schools do occurs during the periods of flat performance, *not* during periods when performance is visibly improving. Periods of visible improvements in performance usually occur as a consequence of earlier investments in knowledge and skill.

SURVIVING THE SLUMPS

Periods of flat performance in the improvement cycle raise some of the most difficult challenges educators face. It feels horrible when you and your colleagues are working harder than you have ever worked, when you have accepted the challenge of incorporating new practices into your work with students, when you are participating in planning and collegial activities that force you to move outside your comfort zone—and you see no visible payoff for these huge investments. These are the periods when it is important to develop a supportive work environment and positive leadership.

We've observed several practices in schools that thrive through stages of flat performance: (1) They expect the flat periods and persist through them; (2) they have a theory about how what they're doing will result in improved student performance; (3) they develop finer-grained measures for detecting improvement; and (4) they make adjustments when evidence suggests that their efforts really aren't working.

Expecting the Flats and Persisting

As schools gain experience with cycles of improvement and stasis (or decline), they recognize that the process of school improvement is the process of uncovering and solving progressively more difficult and challenging problems of student learning, which in turn demand new

Figure 3.1   What School Improvement Really Looks Like

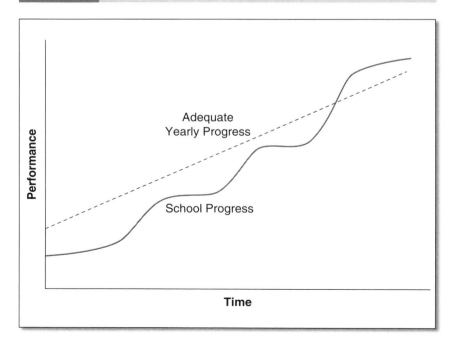

learning from adults. Once the initial gains have reached a plateau, teachers and administrators may begin to focus on a particular set of problems, often associated with broad categories of students, that require deliberate changes in practice.

For example, schools might determine that students are struggling with high-level thinking. One school might respond to this problem by focusing on the tasks teachers are asking students to do every day in the classroom: Are students being asked to do high-level thinking on a regular basis? What do high-level tasks look like in different subjects and grade levels? Another school might respond to the same problem by focusing on questioning: What kinds of questions are teachers asking in class? How might teachers incorporate more high-level questioning into their instruction? Another school might notice that teachers are framing high-level tasks and questions, but not checking to see whether students understand them. This school might focus on appropriate forms of in-class assessment. It takes time for these new practices to mature and become part of the working repertoire of teachers and administrators. Schools that are improving recognize and allow for this time and don't switch gears if they don't see immediate results on state tests.

Having a Theory

It's a lot easier to stay the course if the course is something you anticipated. As educators gain experience, they are more able to explain how what they're doing will lead to the results they want and choose professional development approaches accordingly. We've seen this trajectory in schools' use of the professional development strategy of coaching. At first, schools and districts may adopt coaching because it's a popular strategy and they think that teachers need support around instruction, which coaches can provide. Coaching often doesn't provide the hoped-for outcomes, however, until the school can articulate a theory about *how* the coaching is supposed to help. For example, if the theory is that coaching helps by modeling good instruction and that teachers who see this instruction will adopt that practice, which will then lead to student learning—all that is examinable. Does the teacher's practice change after the modeling? Is there evidence of a difference in student learning? Having a theory also helps identify what improvements to look for in the gap between working hard and seeing state test results, so that you know whether to persist or change course. (For the record, our experience is that modeling alone rarely leads to change in instructional practice, but the point here is to have a theory that both shapes what form your action takes and is testable.)

Developing Finer-Grained Measures for Detecting Improvement

In our experience, changes in student performance lag behind changes in the quality of instructional practice. Improvements are typically visible in classrooms before they show up on external measures. Improvement is not always as obvious as we would like, in part because we look in the wrong places (annual state tests rather than the daily work of teachers and students in classrooms); in part because we use tools that are designed to detect big changes, rather than the tiny ones that lead to the big ones (the equivalent of using a clock with no second hand to measure improvement in the speed at which you can run a mile); and in part because sometimes things get a little worse before they get better. We see this last pattern frequently when teachers go from asking students questions to which there is a correct answer to asking questions for which there are multiple possible answers. At first teachers aren't very good at asking the questions or setting up a classroom environment in which ambiguity and intellectual risk-taking are valued, and students aren't very good at providing answers that require sentences rather than two-word responses or at offering rationales for their answers.

Visible measures of progress are critical for motivating and encouraging educators to persist in the challenging work of improvement. Even the most dedicated and optimistic among us will stop if there's no sign that what we're doing is making a difference or might make a difference eventually.

Making Adjustments

In fact, schools that are improving do stop if there's no sign that what they're doing is making a difference. Having a theory and the right tools to test it makes it possible to identify the need for adjustments. Improving schools are willing to make adjustments, including stopping a course of action, if over time the evidence suggests their strategy isn't working.

THE NEXT LEVEL OF WORK

Sometimes, however, schools aren't sure what adjustments to make. What should schools do when they get stuck? "Stuckness" typically happens when people feel like they are doing their best work and it's not paying off in visible evidence of improved student performance. Billie Jean King—perennial tennis champion and accomplished coach—describes the transformation that occurred in her own career when she learned to regard errors as "feedback." This turned her frustration into reflection, and her reflection into increased focus and correction. Evidence that our best efforts are not producing what we want them to produce is feedback. The evidence is trying to tell us something about what we are doing, and if we listen to it, reflect on it, and give it voice, it will help us understand what to do next.

In our work, we help practitioners frame the next level of work by examining what they are currently doing, looking at evidence of student learning for clues about what is strongest in their practice and where they might see opportunities for improvement, strengthening the capacity of colleagues to work collectively on instructional issues, and increasing the specificity, or "grain size," of the instructional practices they are working on.

It is not unusual for schools to be doing very good work in a given content area—math or literacy—and for that work to be manifested in visible improvements in student performance. As time passes, however, teachers and administrators discover that what they considered to be their "best" work is not reaching certain students or that performance overall is stuck in the middle range and not moving into the advanced range. These kinds of problems typically require closer examination of what students who are doing their "best" work are actually doing. What teachers typically discover is that the actual tasks that students are being asked to do, while considerably more challenging than those they were previously asked to do, are not at a level that will lead to the kind of student performance that teachers hope for. Or they find that the tasks are challenging, but the work is not scaffolded in a way that allows students to reach higher levels of performance. Or they find that students in some classrooms are able to do challenging tasks, but comparable students in other classrooms are not. The next level of work in each of these situations is different.

IMPROVEMENT AND ACCOUNTABILITY

As schools improve, three different but related processes are occurring. First, the level of knowledge and skill that teachers and administrators bring to the work of instructional practice is increasing. Second, teaching is moving from an individual to a collective activity, and internal accountability—the level of agreement and alignment across classrooms around powerful practices—is increasing. Finally, the school is aligning its organizational resources around support for instructional improvement.

All of these processes take time. And, as noted above, they do not occur in a straightforward, linear way. Just as with individual students, individual schools really do differ in the challenges they face and in their capacity to incorporate new practices.

Our accountability systems, as they are currently designed and implemented, do not reflect the real demands of school improvement. Well-designed accountability systems would start from an empirical knowledge of what school improvement looks like when it's happening and establish incentives and supports that accord with that knowledge. At the moment, the process is reversed: Accountability systems establish arbitrary timetables and impose powerful negative incentives on school improvement without any grounding in knowledge of how the process occurs. People in schools are forced to invent the knowledge themselves and must often work against the structures and incentives of the accountability system in order to get the job done.

The discipline of school improvement lies in developing strong internal processes for self-monitoring and reflection—*not* in meeting an artificially imposed schedule of improvement. That existing accountability systems don't reflect this reality is one of the great political tragedies of current education policy.

So, how long does it take? Educators know deep down that this is not the right question because it implies a finish line or a summit that we will someday reach. But that's not how improvement works. Some days we may feel like Sisyphus, forever pushing the boulder up the mountain, never to reach the top. But other days we get to what we thought was the summit and realize that still greater things are possible, things we couldn't see from below.

This is why we teach and lead. Improvement, after all, is essentially learning.

For Further Information

Elmore, R. F. (2005). *School reform from the inside out: Policy, practice, and performance.* Cambridge, MA: Harvard Education Press.

Sebring, P. B., Allensworth, E., Bryk, A. S., Easton, J. Q., & Luppescu, S. (2006). *The essential supports for school improvement.* Chicago: Consortium on Chicago School Research. Available online at http://ccsr.uchicago.edu/content/publications.php?pub_id=86

Wagner, T., Kegan, R., Lahey, L. L., & Lemons, R. W. (2006). *Change leadership: A practical guide to transforming our schools.* San Francisco: Jossey-Bass.

CHAPTER FOUR

The Fourth Way of Change

Andy Hargreaves

Dennis Shirley

Successive waves of social and education reform have been fundamentally flawed. It's time for something bolder and better.

Have you come to believe that standardization and accountability are here to stay? Does it seem that education leaders have little choice but to be compliance officers and data managers who tweak test performance and enforce the latest mandates? If so, think again. Consider the following snapshots of change:

- A high-profile group of business and education leaders, which includes two former U.S. secretaries of education, complains that the U.S. education system has become obsessed with testing basic skills. The group calls for a complete overhaul of current assessment practices (New Commission on the Skills of the American Workforce, 2007).
- Singapore urges its educators to "Teach Less, Learn More" and mandates that all teachers must have 10% of their time free to come up with independent lessons designed to enhance student motivation and creativity.
- In Britain's Celtic fringe (in contrast to England, whose students are the most tested in the world), Scotland continues

to resist standardized testing, Wales has abolished all state testing up to age 14, and Northern Ireland is preparing to abandon the selective exams students take at age 11.

- None of the Nordic countries, which are among the highest performers on the Program for International Student Assessment (PISA), even has an indigenous term for *accountability*. Instead, these countries speak of *collective responsibility* (Hargreaves, Halász, & Pont, 2007).

What does all this mean? Education policy is undergoing a global transformation, and the United States isn't getting it. The United States is not only losing—it's not even playing the right game.

The public, the education profession, and key players in the corporate and philanthropic sectors all sense that something is dreadfully amiss. Only 15% of U.S. educators believe that No Child Left Behind (NCLB) is improving public education (Public Agenda, 2006). Representative George Miller, chair of the House Education and Labor Committee, has abandoned hope for NCLB's reauthorization in the remaining months of the Bush administration, describing the act as "the most negative brand in America" (Hoff, 2007). Middle-class parents are aghast at the loss of play and pleasure in their children's schooling (Tyre, 2006). With more than 70% of school districts reporting they have cut time in social studies, science, foreign languages, and the arts so they can increase attention to tested subjects like math and literacy, it's no surprise that the public is turning against NCLB (Rose & Gallup, 2007).

In England, improvements in achievement results have largely hit a plateau. Most of the gains have been exposed as statistical artifacts and consequences of test preparation (MacBeath et al., 2007). Rates of reading for pleasure are in decline (Offsted Publications Centre, 2004). The majority of English parents are opposed to the current levels of testing for young children (Shaw, 2004), and the education profession is becoming increasingly assertive about the proliferation of interminable inspections and countless tests.

The evidence is clear: Our single-minded focus on achievement gains has not improved the lives of our children. The United States and the United Kingdom occupy the bottom two rungs in United Nations International Children's Emergency Fund's (UNICEF) 2007 survey of child well-being in 21 industrialized countries.

Tested standardization is a political solution in search of the wrong problems. We need better solutions to the problems we actually have and the new challenges we will face in the future.

THE WAY IT WAS

In 1997, President Bill Clinton and Prime Minister Tony Blair convened a group of international leaders to chart a new direction for social policy, which they called the Third Way. Their guru was leading British public intellectual Anthony Giddens, who argued that policymakers needed to move away from the unproductive debate between overdependency on the state (the First Way) and overreliance on free markets (the Second Way).

Giddens (1998) articulated his theory in *The Third Way: The Renewal of Social Democracy*. The First Way, he said, was the welfare state, which in the United States culminated in the Great Society initiatives of the 1960s. These policies provided unprecedented levels of support for the poor, but they also fostered long-term state dependency without providing any real foundation for long-term civic engagement. The First Way granted state professionals, including educators, considerable freedom. In education, it fostered innovation but also allowed unacceptable variations in quality.

In the Second Way, the pendulum swung back. The antitax governments of Ronald Reagan and Margaret Thatcher cut many social services and outsourced others to the private sector. These reforms reduced costs and dependency and encouraged entrepreneurial drive and individual responsibility, but they also undermined social cohesion and widened the gaps between rich and poor. In education, the Second Way manifested itself in increased regulation by the market and the state, leading to a collapse of professional motivation and crises of teacher retention and leadership renewal. High-stakes standardization, driven by government performance targets, sucked the passion and pleasure out of teaching and increased the workload and vulnerability of education leaders (Hargreaves, 2003).

The Third Way, endorsed by Clinton and Blair, offered something between and beyond the first two. It called for increased support for public services in terms of financial resources, buildings, materials, and training. In education, it proposed a mixed economy of diverse providers, leading to the increasing prominence of charter schools in the United States and specialist schools in the United Kingdom. In the Third Way, there has been an encouraging growth of professional communities and networks in which educators and schools share knowledge and help one another improve, thus injecting lateral energy into the system (Fullan, 2006). These are good things.

But there have been disturbing developments, too. A new kind of autocratic and all-seeing state has emerged—one that enforces inflexible government mandates, such as NCLB's adequate yearly progress goals. Although bottom-up support and lateral networks have had some success in securing short-term test gains, the political culture of high-stakes testing is undermining longer-term, more innovative efforts. Political targets in tested basics still drive the hurried interactions of data-driven professional learning communities as teachers anticipate the upcoming test dates in their preparations, curriculum focus, training choices, and classroom activities.

THE WAY IT MIGHT BE

A Nationwide Vision

Other paths to change are possible. On a national level, consider Finland. After being one of the most backward economies in Europe in the 1950s, and after an international banking crisis, the loss of its Russian market, and the escalation of unemployment rates to almost 19% in the early 1990s, Finland consciously coordinated economic and educational transformation. The nation's effort to develop a creative and flexible knowledge economy was accompanied by the development of a significantly more decentralized education system. Finland now has a largely local curriculum and virtually no standardized testing.

Finns control teacher quality at the most important point—the point of entry. Applicants to teacher education programs have only a 1 in 10 chance of acceptance. Even though teacher pay is only average for industrialized nations, teacher retention is high because conditions are good. Within broad guidelines, highly qualified teachers create curriculum together in each municipality for the students they know best. The sense of delivering a curriculum devised by others from afar is utterly alien to Finnish teachers.

In classes rarely larger than 20, Finnish teachers know their students well. Teachers are free from excessive paperwork and endless external activities. They receive generous specialist support as needed. With these advantages, teachers strive for quality by quietly lifting all students up one at a time.

Principals share resources across schools and feel responsible for all the students in their town and city, not only for those in their own school. In each school, the principal is seen as part of a "society of equals," not as a line manager. All principals teach for at least two hours a week. They are often recruited from within their schools; in fact, it is illegal for a principal to be recruited from outside education.

Assessments are largely diagnostic and internal to the school. External accountability is confidential and undertaken on a sample basis for monitoring purposes only, not to impose sanctions on individual students, educators, or schools.

The results: Finland is the world's number-one performer in literacy, math, and science in the PISA rankings for 15-year-old students. It boasts some of the narrowest achievement gaps in the world. It also ranks at or near the top in economic competitiveness (Hargreaves, Halász, & Pont, 2007).

Networking for Power

There are also some leading-edge developments within the Anglo-American community of nations. We recently completed a study of the Raising Achievement, Transforming Learning (RATL) network in England, which comprises more than 300 underperforming secondary schools (Hargreaves, Shirley, Evans, Johnson, & Riseman, 2007). This network articulated a menu of short-term, medium-term, and long-term strategies that education leaders could deploy to meet their goals. Through a system of mentor schools, peer coaching, and reciprocal observation and feedback, as well as a careful study of data to inform but not drive instruction, RATL boosted achievement in more than 200 of its schools at twice the average annual rate.

Although RATL still had a tendency to focus too much on the short term because of the surrounding policy pressures for targets and testing, the power of network-driven improvement—in which professionals support and challenge professionals, schools work with schools, and the strong help the weak—provides powerful clues about the elements of a

Fourth Way strategy that can drive improvement. Indeed, the network is now pushing beyond immediate results into more profound transformations: for example, cultivating pupils as leaders of change, engaging community members in discussions of how culture and language can support improvement, and radically altering the curriculum to accommodate the visual learning styles of some students.

Systemic Change Arising From Communities

Not all reform starts with government. A report by the Annenberg Institute for School Reform (Mediratta et al., 2008) provides valuable new evidence of the power of bottom-up reforms for raising pupil achievement, even in the face of top-down accountability systems. The research team studied seven urban school districts and targeted schools that were working closely with community-based organizations. Findings included the following:

- People Acting for Community Together in Miami matched parents with partner schools to focus on literacy instruction in elementary schools. The percentage of 3rd- and 4th-grade students achieving proficiency in reading on the Florida Comprehensive Assessment Test improved from 27% in 2001 to 49% in 2005, far outpacing a comparison set of demographically similar schools.
- Among schools affiliated with the Industrial Areas Foundation in Austin, Texas, those with higher levels of faculty engagement showed larger percentages of students meeting minimum standards on the Texas state test.
- A campaign by the Oakland Community Organization divided that city's largest and most dysfunctional high schools into small schools. The new schools showed improved graduation rates, increased enrollment in college-preparatory coursework, and improved ratings on California's Academic Performance Index.

Perhaps the most interesting finding was that community organizing is correlated with higher levels of teacher-parent trust, sense of school community and safety, achievement-oriented culture, and parent involvement in the school.

Toward a Fourth Way

The First Way of the welfare state had a sense of mission and showed the value of innovation but resulted in too much variation in quality and implementation. The Second Way of markets and standardization provided urgency, consistency, and direction, but at great cost to professional motivation, authentic achievement, and curriculum creativity. The Third Way has increased levels of support and added lateral professional energy but subjected teachers to a frantic and frenetic pursuit of arbitrary improvement targets.

Each way had strengths in some areas but enormous limitations in others. We propose a Fourth Way of change—informed by an effort to identify and learn from the best of the past, enlightened by high-performance exemplars like Finland in the present, and inspired by a commitment to more innovative and inclusive goals for the future. The Fourth Way would rest on five pillars of purpose and partnership, three principles of professionalism, and four catalysts of coherence.

Pillars of Purpose

The solid pillars of purpose and partnership that uphold the edifice of the Fourth Way include

- *An inspiring and inclusive vision* that draws people together in pursuit of an uplifting common purpose.
- *Deepened public engagement* that harnesses and legitimizes the proven power of community organizing to inspire a great public debate about the future of education.
- *Achievement through increased investment* in education facilities and other social services, confirming the First Way's emphasis on our shared social responsibility to support and create better opportunities for the poor.
- *Corporate educational responsibility,* with education and business partners equally accountable to each other.
- *Students as partners in change* rather than merely targets of change efforts and services—more involved in their own learning and learning choices, actively consulted about the quality and improvement of teaching, and substantially engaged in the overall governance of the school and its development.

Principles of Professionalism

Education leaders and teachers are the ultimate arbiters of change. The classroom door is the portal to reform or the raised drawbridge that holds it at bay. Three principles of professionalism are indispensable components of any sustainable change:

- *High-quality teachers* who are attracted by their country's inspiring and inclusive vision; have high status as builders of their nation's future; enjoy supportive working conditions, sufficient pay, and professional autonomy; and are trained to a rigorous intellectual and practical standard.
- *Powerful professionalism* in which teachers' associations become profound agents of systemic change that benefits students, not only opponents or implementers of changes imposed on them by others.
- *Lively learning communities* in which teachers learn and improve together in cultures of collaboration, trust, and responsibility.

Catalysts of Coherence

The hardest part of any plan for change in education is how to make it spread. *Coherence* does not mean cloning or aligning everything so it looks the same in all schools. It means bringing diverse people together to work skillfully and effectively for a common cause that lifts them up and moves them in the same direction. Four catalysts can create this coherence:

- *Sustainable leadership* that is integral to educational change, not an afterthought. One way to build more leadership capacity is to increase supply by identifying and developing aspiring and emerging leaders. But we can also increase capacity by reducing unnecessary demand—eliminating the excessive reform demands that deter many qualified potential leaders and trusting them to become inspirational developers of their communities instead of mere managers of imposed targets and external initiatives. Where Singapore now advises "Teach Less, Learn More," we would add "Reform Less, Improve More."
- *Networks of mutual learning.* As in England's leading-edge Raising Achievement, Transforming Learning project,

schools must support and learn from one another, become collectively responsible for all the children and youth in their city or community, and commit to systems and dispositions where the strong help the weak.

- *Responsibility before accountability.* As in Finland, we must give a higher priority to collective professional responsibility than to external accountability. And we must base external accountability on sampling rather than a politically distorted insistence on testing every student.
- *Building from the bottom, steering from the top.* Social policy should neither let a thousand flowers bloom nor micromanage everything in detail, but rather provide a broad and inspired sense of direction with genuine development of community and professional responsibility. Positive change should emerge and spread from below rather than being dictated from the top.

A NEW VISION

With Barack Obama's presidency, Americans have new opportunities to reshape education policy. Obama and Secretary of Education Arne Duncan recognize that something has gone terribly wrong with the NCLB accountability machine, which is now spitting nuts and bolts all over the boiler room floor.

The theories behind the First, Second, and Third Ways that have defined recent U.S. education strategy have been fundamentally flawed. Now it is time for something bolder and better. We need to let leaders lead again. We need to engage the public, not just submit citizens to opinion polls and electioneering. And with lateral learning networks spreading within and across schools, we need to put educators themselves at the leading edge of reform.

Most of all, we need a vision of education as a public good that shapes the future of all of us. This vision should help us develop greater innovation and creativity, expect and demand commitment and perseverance from our students, foster the international awareness and cultural understanding that strengthen global partnerships and security, and promote the inclusiveness that elevates our differences into the strengths that can enable us to bring about opportunity for all in a just society.

In the Fourth Way, there will still be standards, including public, human, and ethical ones, but there will no longer be standardization. There will be hard work and persistence, but not pointless drudgery. There will be greater support for the education profession, but not unconditionally. The goal of the Fourth Way is to create the schools that will undergird and catalyze our best values to regenerate and improve society. Only then will the United States become the education leader that others around the globe eagerly seek.

REFERENCES

Fullan, M. (2006). *Turnaround leadership.* San Francisco: Jossey-Bass.

Giddens, A. (1998). *The third way: The renewal of social democracy.* Cambridge, UK: Policy Press.

Hargreaves, A. (2003). *Teaching in the knowledge society: Education in the age of insecurity.* New York: Teachers College Press.

Hargreaves, A., Halász, G., & Pont, B. (2007). *School leadership for systemic improvement in Finland.* Paris: OECD.

Hargreaves, A., Shirley, D., Evans, M., Johnson, C., & Riseman, D. (2007). *The long and short of school improvement: Final evaluation of the Raising Achievement, Transforming Learning programme of the Specialist Schools and Academies Trust.* London: Specialist Schools and Academies Trust.

Hoff, D. J. (2007). "Growth models" gaining in accountability debate. *Education Week, 27*(16), 22–25.

MacBeath, J., Gray, J., Cullen, J., Frost, D., Steward, S., & Swaffield, S. (2007). *Schools on the edge: Responding to challenging circumstances.* London: Paul Chapman.

Mediratta, K., Shah, S., McAlister, S., Fruchter, N., Mokhtar, C., & Lockwood, D. (2008). *Organized communities, stronger schools: A preview of research findings.* Providence, RI: Annenberg Institute for School Reform.

New Commission on the Skills of the American Workforce. (2007). *Tough choices, tough times.* Washington, DC: National Center on Education and the Economy.

Offsted Publications Centre. (2004). *Reading for purpose and pleasure: An evaluation of the teaching of reading in primary schools.* London: Crown.

Public Agenda. (2006). *Reality check 2006: Issue no. 3: Is support for standards and testing fading?* New York: Author.

Rose, L. C., & Gallup, A. M. (2007, September). The 39th annual Phi Delta Kappan/Gallup poll of the public's attitudes toward the public schools.

Phi Delta Kappan, 89(1), 33–48. Available online at www.pdkmem
bers.org/members_online/publications/e-GALLUP/kpoll_pdfs/pdkpo
ll39_2007.pdf

Shaw, M. (2004, April 9). End testing of infants: Seven is too young for tests
say parents in TES poll. *London Times Educational Supplement,* p. 1.

Tyre, P. (2006, September 11). The new first grade: Too much too soon.
Newsweek, pp. 34–44.

UNICEF. (2007). *Child poverty in perspective: An overview of child well-
being in rich countries, Innocenti Report Card 7.* Florence: UNICEF
Innocenti Research Centre.

CHAPTER FIVE

Transforming High Schools

Lessons Learned From Recent Reforms

Pedro A. Noguera

As educators have experimented and grappled with various strategies for raising student achievement, it has become increasingly clear that we face our biggest challenges in our efforts to improve public high schools. Steeped in tradition and reliant on practices that have long outlived their usefulness, many of our nation's high schools are in dire need of reform, but so far, many efforts have proved unsuccessful at transforming this venerable American institution. While there are numerous examples of elementary schools that have been turned around—from low performing to high achieving schools—there are relatively few examples of high schools that have undergone a similar transformation.

The problems confronting high schools show up in affluent suburbs and rural areas, but, as is true with most educational issues, the failings are most acute in urban neighborhoods where poverty is concentrated. Drop-out rates in many urban districts, especially for African Americans and Latinos, are high, often over 50%, even though they are typically underreported (National Education Association, 2001; Education Trust, 2002). The advent of No Child Left Behind (NCLB) and the high-stakes exit exams that have been instituted by states as requirements for graduation have contributed to large numbers of students being retained in the ninth grade

(Haney, 2003) and many more forced to leave high school without a diploma (Civil Rights Project, 2000). Additionally, many high schools are plagued by violence and bullying, vandalism and gang activity, poor attendance, low teacher morale, and an inability to attract and retain strong principals. These problems are by no means limited to high schools but available evidence indicates that they are more common there (Aspen Institute, 2001).

Over the last 10 years, several national studies have attempted to diagnose the causes of the problems that beset so many American high schools in the hope that by identifying the source of the troubles it might be possible to devise a strategy for reform. The findings from this research reveals

1. High schools suffer from a variety of organizational flaws including fragmentation, insufficient attention to quality control in programs and services, and a lack of coherence in mission (Annenberg Foundation, 2003).

2. The school curriculum typically offers a broad but disconnected variety of courses that lack depth and intellectual rigor (Powell & Cohen, 1985).

3. The quality of teaching and a tendency on the part of teachers to rely on lecture and emphasize delivery of content without looking for evidence of learning or mastery of knowledge and skills (Aspen Institute, 2001).

4. Student alienation, boredom, strained relationships between adults and students, and an anti-intellectual peer culture are pervasive and undermine efforts to raise academic achievement (Bryk, 2002; Steinberg, 1996).

5. Too many schools are simply too large and overcrowded to provide students with the support and attention they need (Ayers & Klonsky, 2000).

With so much evidence that something had to be done to overhaul American high schools, several public and private organizations have in recent years initiated a number of costly and far-reaching reforms. In the last 10 years, millions of dollars have been invested by the Bill and Melinda Gates Foundation, which has emerged as the leader of the effort to improve high schools through the development of smaller, and in some cases, autonomous learning communities. Similar initiatives have been funded by the Carnegie, Brode, and Annenberg foundations. More recently, the U.S. Department of Education has begun funding efforts to restructure and reduce the size of secondary schools. Though the efficacy of many of the reform strategies remains largely unknown, large sums of money are being allocated to school districts across the country to support the effort to transform American secondary schools.

PATHWAYS TO STUDENT SUCCESS

Well aware of the challenges and the failure of past reforms, I decided to study the reform process itself in order to understand why high schools had proved so difficult to change and improve. After moving from Berkeley to Cambridge in the fall of 2000, I decided to undertake research on high school reform in Boston where several major initiatives among the public high schools were already underway. When I arrived, the district had already spent several years and substantial sums of money on efforts aimed at improving its high schools. While the track record of these efforts was mixed, it was clear that at several of the most troubled schools much of what the district had attempted was not working. The district's needs combined with my past experience as a teacher and researcher in high schools prompted me to immerse myself in the effort to tackle the problems facing the city's secondary schools.

As was true in many cities across the country, Boston had experimented with a variety of strategies to reform its high schools. In the early 1990s, Boston Public Schools (BPS) established several pilot schools (district schools that function with the flexibility of charter schools), many of which were quite successful. Pilots had been created with the hope that greater flexibility and autonomy would enable these schools to serve as test sites for innovative practice. However, even though they were part of the district, their special status resulted in them being resented by the more traditional schools, and very little communication occurred among leaders from different types of schools. There were also several charter schools in

Boston that sprang up over the previous decade, and though their advocates claimed their presence would create competition for traditional schools and compel them to improve (Elmore, 1996), within the district there was even less communication or awareness of what they were doing.

Given the lack of knowledge about alternative models and given the glaring problems confronting so many of the district's traditional secondary schools, I thought that a comparative study of high schools might be most helpful. In consultation with the district Superintendent, Tom Payzant, and other BPS administrators, a plan to study high schools and the reforms that were at various stages of implementation was devised. The goal was to learn more about the process of change by studying how specific reforms were affecting the experience of students. Such an approach seemed to make the most sense given that changing student behavior, particularly with respect to academic performance, was ostensibly the primary objective of the reform efforts. We also hoped that such a study would make it possible to extract some lessons from several years of reform that might prove useful to other schools in other districts across the country.

Pathways for Student Success (PSS) was launched in the fall of 2001 with funding from the National Science Foundation, the Nellie Mae Foundation, and the Schott Family Foundation. Ten schools representing the different types of high schools that were operating in the city were selected for participation in the study. These included four comprehensive schools (one of which had a vocational focus), three pilot schools, two charter schools, and one exam school (an academic magnet school at which students must qualify in order to be admitted). We worked with site leaders to select a sample that was as representative as possible in terms of race, gender, and language of the overall population, and at each school approximately fifteen 10th-grade students (five high achievers, five midlevel, and five low) (N=150) were recruited to participate in the study. Our intention was to collect a variety of data on each of these students: observing them in and outside of the classroom, interviewing their teachers and parents, and examining their school records. By studying their experiences as closely as possible, we hoped to gain insights into the ways in which their academic performance and social development were being affected by various reforms.

High Stakes Testing

At the time we carried out this research the most significant and far reaching of the reforms being implemented was standards-based accountability. The graduating class of 2003 was the first to be required to pass the state exit exam, MCAS (Massachusetts Comprehensive Assessment System), in order to graduate, and each of the tenth graders in our sample was required to take the exam in the Spring. Threatened with the prospect that large numbers of their students might not receive diplomas, all of the schools in the study were under intense pressure to find ways to prepare their students.

Given that the stakes were so high, what we learned about how schools were preparing their students was both surprising and troubling. On the surface, it appeared as though the schools were doing all they could to ensure that their students, especially their seniors, were ready for the state exam in order to limit the number of students who would fail. For example, at several of the schools, students who had failed the exam once or more were enrolled in double-period test preparation courses modeled after the type of Princeton Review courses used to help students to study for the SAT. However, as we looked closely at these courses we soon discovered that at most of the schools there was no focus on quality control. In many of the classes we visited the courses were disorganized, poorly managed, and in several cases taught by teachers who lacked the knowledge and skills to teach the material. For example, in one language arts course that had been set up for students who had failed the exam on two occasions, students informed us that for three months they were taught by a substitute teacher who took attendance and spent most of his time reading the newspaper. When we informed the principal of this situation, she let us know that she was aware of the problem but said there was nothing she could do until the regular teacher returned from maternity leave.

This was just one of several examples of short cuts schools were using to boost scores. In many of the schools it was clear that they were hoping to raise student scores without ensuring that students had been exposed to the material covered on the exam or without improving the quality of teaching provided at the school. For example, as we examined the school records of students in our sample, we noticed that several of the students who had failed the math portion of the exam had failed algebra and had not taken any higher-level math courses. To be fully prepared for the math portion of the MCAS, a student should have taken three years of college prep math: algebra, geometry, and algebra II. At many of the schools in our study, only a limited number of sections of advanced math were offered, and few if any 10th graders had completed this course sequence.[1] Moreover, in private conversations with many of the principals at the schools, several admitted that they lacked a sufficient number of teachers who could actually teach the material covered on the exam. In one of the most ironic experiences I had when reporting findings from the research after the first year, I informed one of the principals that the students in our sample believed their teachers had very low expectations of them. Shaking his head with disgust, he responded, "I know this is a problem, but I can't deal with it until I find a way to raise the test scores." Recognizing that efforts to improve the quality of teaching would take years to bear fruit, the most common response to high-stakes testing was to teach students who were behind academically test-taking skills. Given that at some of the schools nearly half of the seniors failed the MCAS and therefore did not receive a diploma, it was clear that this strategy was not very effective.

Small Learning Communities

Several schools were also experimenting with other reforms, such as the development of small learning communities (SLCs), block scheduling, new systems for advising students, and at some schools, the utilization of a more integrated curriculum. The thinking behind these reforms was that structural changes, such as reducing the size of the school or lengthening class periods, would make it possible to provide students with a more personalized learning environment. It was hoped that a more intimate learning environment would in turn lead to improved student-teacher relationships and that higher levels of achievement would follow. At some of the schools,

---

1. One of the major problems with the way in which Massachusetts and several other states have designed and implemented standards-based reform is that state government has done very little to ensure that schools are able to provide their students with the academic preparation to meet the high standards embodied in the exams.

these small learning communities were organized around curricular themes (i.e., communications, technology, business), while at others efforts were made to minimize differences between SLCs. To support the goals of this change, many of the schools also adopted a new advising system that called upon teachers to serve as counselors of students through an extended homeroom period held once per week.

The rationale behind these changes seemed to make sense. There was evidence from the research literature that student alienation and a lack of engagement was a problem that contributed to low achievement (Wasley et al., 2000; Newman, 1992), and several studies suggested that these kinds of reforms could help in addressing the problem. However, as we looked closely at how the reforms were being implemented, once again we saw a tremendous gap between the intent of the reforms and its effects on students.

For example, at several of the schools, the only people who knew they were in an SLC and who seemed to clearly understand the goals and purpose of the reform were the administrators responsible for running them. In part, this is because the changes introduced were relatively new; most SLCs had been in operation for three years or less, and most had not yet found a way to create a sense of community or common identity for students or teachers within the new smaller schools. However, interviews with teachers and students also revealed that aside from changing the courses they had access to and who they took classes with, the SLCs had actually done very little to transform the schools. Closer examination revealed that the creation of SLCs had not resulted in improved relations between teachers and students, greater academic engagement, or higher achievement.

One of the questions we posed to students at all of the schools was, "Is there an adult at your school who you would turn to if you were experiencing a serious personal problem?" With the exception of two of the schools I will return to later, over 80% of the students at the other eight schools reported that there was no adult they felt comfortable discussing a personal problem with. We also asked students if they felt their teachers were concerned about how well they did in school, and disturbingly, 56% said they did not. These findings are similar to findings from several national student surveys (Metropolitan Life, 2002). However, what is troubling about this consistency is that it suggests that the effort to reduce the size of high schools, a major reform being carried out in many high schools across the United States, may not be producing the results that are hoped for.

We also sat in on several advisory classes where no advising was occurring because teachers had no idea of how to make use of the allotted time and most lacked experience with counseling. It was also clear that in most of the schools the adoption of SLCs had not been accompanied by a change in the quality of instruction students received. Even in the schools that had adopted longer periods as part of a new block schedule, we typically found the same approach to teaching—heavy reliance on lecture and passive learning that is common to most traditional high schools. We observed several classrooms where students were sleeping, putting on makeup, or assigned to watch films that were unrelated to the course content. During a visit to one of the schools, we were told by a student that if we went with him to class his teacher would not allow the students to play cards as they normally do. To our surprise and dismay, even with two researchers seated in the back of the classroom, the students were allowed to play cards for the entire class period while the teacher presented an assignment to a small group of students seated at the front of the room.

The newness of the reforms and the inordinate pressure that many of the administrators were under due to budget cuts and high stakes testing is undoubtedly part of the reason for the poor implementation of the reforms and the lack of alignment between the claims of the administrators and the effects on students. Yet, our research at the 10 schools left me with little reason to believe that there would be greater improvement over time. At some of the schools, there was a willingness to use findings generated from the research to modify reform plans, however, at the most troubled schools, administrators were more likely to say that they were under too much pressure to use the information. Sadly, there is no sign that the pressure the principals have been under will decrease, and without a commitment to quality control in program delivery, there is little reason to believe that the schools will improve. Even more disturbing is the limited ability of administrators to institute reforms that have an impact on teaching and learning in the classroom. It continues to be the case that many administrators assume changes in the organizational structure of schools—block scheduling, advisories, small learning communities—will result in changes in the classroom, even though there is no evidence that this is the case. Research on school reform has shown that this rarely occurs (Fullan & Miles, 1992) and that only a strategy focused on improving instruction will lead to lasting improvements in teaching and learning (Elmore, 1996).

Laser-like focus on teaching and learning is precisely what we saw at the two schools in the study that were experiencing the greatest success. I turn now to a description of these schools in order to extract lessons that might prove helpful to efforts to improve high schools.

LEARNING FROM SUCCESS

At two of the schools in the Pathways study—one a pilot, the other a charter—the reforms that were implemented appeared directly related to higher levels of student achievement. Interestingly, both of these were relatively small schools—the pilot had 330 students, and the charter had 226—and both had specific requirements for admission intended not to screen out students but to let them know they would have to meet high standards and expectations. These features did not set these schools apart from the others in the study. There were others that were smaller and some that were more selective, but these as well as other features influenced the unique culture of these schools and served to distinguished them from the others.

For example, at both schools students were required to work harder and, in some cases, longer. The charter had a longer school day (9:00 a.m.–4:30 p.m.) and school year (school ended after the first week of July), while the pilot required a portfolio assessment and a junior and senior project in addition to the state exit exam. Both schools had also gone to great lengths to develop unique school cultures. The charter school was organized around an Asian theme and students were required to study Mandarin and martial arts. Although relatively small, the pilot school was divided into three small learning communities, and students spent significant amounts of time in community-based internships. Both schools were very attentive to the needs of their teachers and made on-site professional development available throughout the school year designed around a curriculum that was informed by teacher needs. Finally, both schools required a high level of parental involvement and provided students with college advising beginning in the ninth grade.

The greatest evidence that these practices as well as others I haven't mentioned were effective can be seen in both the achievement of their students and the responses of the students to our interview questions. At all 10 of the schools in the study, the majority of students were minority and low income, however, these two schools were the only ones where none of the seniors failed the MCAS. Even more encouraging, at both schools the average student scored at the proficiency level, and several achieved the highest level on the state exam. In contrast to most of the other students at the other schools who reported there were no adults they would speak to about a personal problem, at both of these schools, over 90% of the students said there were (93% of the students at the charter and 100% of the students at the pilot). Similarly, when we asked students whether they felt encouraged to do well at school, responses of both schools' students were uniformly affirmative. In response to this question, one 11th-grader put it this way:

> At _____ school, you have no choice but to work hard. They're on you from the time you first get here. If you don't do your homework they call home, and then they make you do it. You can't get away with nothing here, and after a while you start to realize that everybody's working and it starts to feels good to know that everyone is gonna make it. They make sure that we're all going to college at this school.

CONCLUSION

The contrast between these two high performing schools and the others in the Pathways study was striking. Interestingly, the high performing schools had no secret strategies or special resources that were not available to the other schools. In fact, many of the reforms they pursued were also being implemented at the other schools. What set these schools apart was not what they did but how they did it. Rather than introducing a reform and hoping for the best, these schools took the time to make sure that teachers, parents, and students understood the purpose behind a reform strategy, and equally important, they looked for evidence that the reform was achieving the goals that had been set.

At most of the schools, the most obvious and unfortunate finding was that the adults responsible for implementing reforms were oblivious to the ways in which students were being affected by the changes that had been introduced. The disconnect between the reforms and the student experience seemed attributable to a lack of systematic evaluation and to an unwillingness or failure to recognize the value of seeking input from students. Listening to students to learn more about the effectiveness of our schools is in fact a radical departure from the way schools typically run.

At the suggestion of the students from one of the schools in the study, we brought all 150 students together at Harvard University for a retreat on a Saturday. We divided them into small groups and then posed the following question: If you were to attend a school where you would be excited to learn and study, how would that school be organized? How would you be taught? What would you learn? The students met for two hours, brainstorming response to these questions. As they reported out to the whole group at the end of the day, it became clear that the most consistent theme was that students wanted a more interactive teaching style, a curriculum more relevant to their lives and experience, school rules that were responsive to their living circumstances, and schools that gave them a role and a voice in their own education.

As the students reported their ideas, the Deputy Superintendent of Boston was feverishly taking notes. At one point, I turned to her and asked her what she thought of the students' ideas. She responded, "These are great ideas. I can really use them because it will help us in the work we're doing with the high schools." I pointed out to her that these ideas were in her schools all of the time, and all we needed to do was to find a way to more systematically include them.

Too often, we assume that if the adults do things right, the kids will fall into line. Perhaps, if we were more willing to listen and solicit their opinion, we might find ways to engage them more deeply in their own education. The students may not have the answers to the problems confronting our nation's high schools, but perhaps if we engage them in discussions over how to make school less alienating and more meaningful, together we might find ways to break the cycle of failure.

REFERENCES

Annenberg Foundation. (2003). *Rethinking accountability: Voices in urban education.* Providence, RI: Author.

Aspen Institute. (2001). *Transforming the American high school* (M. Cohen, Ed.). Washington, DC: Author.

Ayers, W., & Klonsky, M. (2000). *A simple justice.* New York: Teachers College Press.

Bryk, A. (2002). *Trust in schools: A core resource for improvement.* New York: Russell Sage Foundation.

Civil Rights Project. (2000). *Implications for high stakes testing in grades K–12.* Cambridge, MA: Harvard University Press.

Education Trust. (2002). *Dispelling the myth: Lessons from high performing schools.* Washington, DC: Education Trust.

Elmore, R. F. (1996). *Restructuring in the classroom.* San Francisco: Jossey Bass.

Fullan, M., & Miles, M. (1992, June). Getting reform right: What works and what doesn't. *Phi Delta Kappan,* 745–752.

Haney, W. (2003). *Attrition of students from New York schools.* Invited testimony at public hearing "Regents Learning Standards and High School Graduation Requirements" before the New York Senate Standing Committee on Education. Retrieved February 16, 2009, from http://www.richgibson.com/rouge_forum/CSSE2008/HurshCSSE 2008.pdf

Metropolitan Life. (2002). *The American teacher.* New York: Author.

National Education Association. (2001). *School dropouts in the United States: A policy discussion.* Washington, DC: Author.

Newman, F. (Ed.). (1992). *Student engagement and achievement in American secondary schools.* New York: Teachers College Press.

Powell, A. G., & Cohen, D. K. (1985). *The shopping mall high school: Winners and losers in the education marketplace.* Boston: Houghton Mifflin.

Steinberg, L. (1996). *Beyond the classroom.* New York: Simon & Schuster.

Wasley, P., Fine, M., Gladden, M., Holland, N., King, S., Mosak, E., Powell, L. (2000). *Small schools, great strides: A study of small schools in Chicago.* New York: Bank Street College of Education.

PART II

Instructional Focus at the School Level

Michael Fullan

As I said in the introduction, considerable progress has been made at the classroom and school level over the past decade. In the first two articles, colleagues and I focus on school leadership and the link to "breakthrough" results that we define as full success in achieving proficiency in literacy and numeracy for virtually all students. The evidence is that this will require shared leadership, a sharp focus on "deprivatizing" classroom teaching in order to get at instructional improvement, deliberate daily use of diagnostic data, and school cultures where all teachers learn how to get better all the time.

DuFour and his colleagues reinforce these notions by showing how "professional learning communities" involve deep and persistent changes in school cultures in order to focus on results through purposeful collaboration.

The work of change leaders is the basis of the final two articles. Knight's piece is on the ever-growing importance of coaches and mentors within schools—what I call "second change agents" (the principal being the first change agent). Then, Leithwood and his colleagues show how to develop and sustain school principals through networks and in individual development.

The work on the school principalship is especially crucial these days as principals are being cast increasingly into the role of school saviors. In my own analysis, the danger is that the role is becoming over-burdened with the combination of managerial and change demands, and therefore action must be taken by principals and by the system to prioritize and support principals (Fullan, 2008).

REFERENCES

Fullan, M. (2008). *What's worth fighting for in the principalship* (2nd ed.). New York: Teachers College Press; Toronto: Ontario Principals' Council.

CHAPTER SIX

The Principal and Change

Michael Fullan

Effective principals attack incoherence.

—*Bryk, Sebring, Kerbow, Rollow,*
and Easton (1998, p. 287)

orget about the principal as head of the school for a moment, and think of her or him as someone just as buffeted as the teacher is by wanted or unwanted and often incomprehensible changes—and, what is more, *expected to lead these very changes.* Change is only one of the forces competing for the principal's attention and usually not the most compelling one. And when it is compelling, as is the case recently, it is difficult to focus and sustain the work needed for reform to be effective. Yet, some principals are actively engaged as initiators or facilitators of continuous improvements in their schools. The principal is in the middle of the relationship between teachers and external ideas and people. As in most human triangles, there are constant conflicts and dilemmas. How the principal approaches (or avoids) these issues determines to a large extent whether these relationships constitute a Bermuda triangle of innovations.

An understanding of what reality is *from the point of view of people within the role* is an essential starting point for constructing a practical theory of the meaning and results of change attempts. This phenomenology is social science's contribution to addressing the frequent lament, "No one understands me." In the field of educational change, everyone feels misunderstood. One of the most revealing and frustrating indicators of the difficulties in educational change is the participants' frequent experience of having their intentions not only misunderstood but also interpreted exactly opposite of what they meant. Principals should have no problem claiming their fair share of frustration, as the role of the principal has become dramatically more complex and overloaded over the past decade. On the optimistic side, very recent research has identified some specific change-related behaviors of principals who deal effectively with educational change. It is time to go beyond the empty phrase, "The principal is the gatekeeper of change."

While research on school improvement is now into its fourth decade, systematic research on what the principal actually does and its relationship to stability and change is quite recent. Some of the earlier implementation research identified the role of the principal as central to promoting or inhibiting change, but it did not examine the principal's role in any depth or perspective. By the 1990s, research had accumulated that put principals front and center in leading improvement at the school and community levels. Today, no serious change effort would fail to emphasize the key role of the principal. Most provide both professional development and altered job descriptions highlighting the role of the principal in leading change on the ground. The irony is that as the change expectations heighten, the *principalship* itself has become overloaded in a way that makes it impossible to fulfill the promise of widespread, sustained reform.

I start with a description of where principals are. I then turn to the part of their role that interests us the most—what principals do and don't do in relation to change. In the last section of the chapter, I talk about the complexity of leadership and offer some guidelines for how principals might lead change more effectively. I also should acknowledge at the outset that effective principals share—in fact, develop—leadership among teachers. So, we are really talking about assistant principals, department heads, grade-level coordinators, and teacher leaders of all types in the school.

WHERE PRINCIPALS ARE

"Pressure drives heads to drink," blares a headline in the *Times Education Supplement* (2000) in England. The article reports that among the principals and deputy principals in the district of

Warwickshire (a district with 250 schools), 40% had visited the doctor with stress-related problems in the past year and 30% were taking medication. Warwickshire was selected, says the article, because it was considered to be a well-run district—a good employer!

With the move toward the self-management of schools, the principal appears to have the worst of both worlds. The old world is still around, with expectations that the principal will run a smooth school and to be responsive to all; simultaneously, the new world rains down on schools with disconnected demands, expecting that at the end of the day the school constantly should be showing better test results and ideally becoming a learning organization.

In *What's Worth Fighting for in the Principalship?* (Fullan, 1997), I reported on a study of 137 principals and vice principals in Toronto. The growing overload experienced by principals was evident over 20 years ago: 90% reported an increase over the previous 5 years in the demands made on their time, including new program demands, the number of board priorities and directives, and the number of directives from the Ministry of Education. Time demands were listed as having increased in dealing with parent and community groups (92% said there was an increase), trustee requests (91%), administration activities (88%), staff involvement and student services (81%), social services (81%), and board initiatives (69%).

Principals and vice principals also were asked about their perceptions of effectiveness: 61% reported a *decrease in principal effectiveness,* with only 13% saying it was about the same, and 26% reporting an increase. The same percentage, 61%, reported decreases in "the effectiveness of assistance from immediate superiors and from administration." Further, 84% reported a decrease in the authority of the principal; 72%, a decrease in trust in leadership of the principal; and 76%, a decrease in principal involvement in decision making at the system level. To the question, "Do you think the principal can effectively fulfill all the responsibilities assigned to him/her?" 91% responded, "No" (Fullan, 1997, p. 2).

The discouragement felt by principals in attempting to cover all the bases is aptly described in the following three responses from interviews conducted by Duke (1998) with principals who were considering quitting.

> The conflict for me comes from going home every night acutely aware of what didn't get done, and feeling after six years that I ought to have a better batting average than I have.

If you leave the principalship, think of all the "heart-work" you're going to miss. I fear I'm addicted to it and to the pace of the principalship—those 2,000 interactions a day. I get fidgety in meetings because they're too slow, and I'm not out there interacting with people.

The principalship is the kind of job where you're expected to be all things to all people. Early on, if you're successful, you have gotten feedback that you are able to be all things to all people. And then you feel an obligation to continue to do that, which in your own mind you're not capable of doing. And that causes some guilt. (p. 309)

Duke was intrigued by the "drop-out rate" of principals after encountering an article stating that 22% of Vermont administrators employed in the fall of 1984 had left the state's school systems by the fall of 1985. In interviewing principals about why they considered quitting, he found that sources of dissatisfaction included policy and administration, lack of achievement, sacrifices in personal life, lack of growth opportunities, lack of recognition and too little responsibility, relations with subordinates, and lack of support from superiors. They expressed a number of concerns about the job itself: the challenge of doing all the things that principals are expected to do, the mundane or boring nature of much of the work, the debilitating array of personal interactions, the politics of dealing with various constituencies, and the tendency for managerial concerns to supersede leadership functions. Duke suggested that the reasons principals were considering quitting were related to fatigue, awareness of personal limitations, and awareness of the limitation of career choices. Principals experienced reality shock, "the shock-like reactions of new workers when they find themselves in a work situation for which they have spent several years preparing and for which they thought they were going to be prepared, and then suddenly find that they are not." Duke concludes that

A number of frustrations expressed by these principals derived from the contexts in which they worked. Their comments send a clear message to those who supervised them: principals need autonomy *and* support. The need for autonomy may require supervisors to treat each principal differently; the need for support may require supervisors to be sensitive to each principal's view of what he or she finds meaningful or trivial about the work. (p. 312, emphasis in original)

There is no question that the demands on the principalship have become even more intensified over the past 10 years, 5 years, 1 year. More and more principals in almost every Western country are retiring early; more and more potential teacher leaders are concluding that it is simply not worth it to take on the leadership of schools.

Wanted: A miracle worker who can do more with less, pacify rival groups, endure chronic second-guessing, tolerate low levels of support, process large volumes of paper and work double shifts (75 nights a year). He or she will have carte blanche to innovate, but cannot spend much money, replace any personnel, or upset any constituency. (Evans, 1995, p. 5)

Is this an impossible job? A job that is simply not worth the aggravation and toll it takes? Even students, such as this secondary student, notice. *"I* don't think being a head is a good job. You have to work too hard. Some days [the head] looks knackered—sorry, very tired" (Day, Harris, Hadfield, Toley, & Beresford, 2000, p. 126).

At the present time, the principalship is not worth it, and therein lies the solution. If effective principals energize teachers in complex times, what is going to energize principals? We are now beginning to see more clearly examples of school principals who are successful. These insights can help existing principals become more effective; even more, they provide a basis for establishing a system of recruiting, nurturing, and supporting and holding accountable school leaders.

THE PRINCIPAL AND CHANGE

Until recently, the principal was often neglected in the formulation of strategies for reform. As research mounted about the significant impact of the principal, for better or for worse, on reform outcomes, policymakers began to incorporate the role of school leaders in leading change initiatives. This has not proved easy to do and in fact has helped to illuminate the fundamental difficulties of changing school cultures. Let us trace the evolution of this interesting phenomenon over the past decade, and especially the past five years. I know of no improving school that doesn't have a principal who is good at lead-ing improvement. "Almost every single study of school effectiveness has shown both primary and secondary leadership to be a key fac-tor," says Sammons (1999 p. 195) in her major review.

The first half of my argument—to consolidate the case for how and why the principal is crucial for success—is presented in this section. In the following section, I take up the second half of the analysis to show the problems encountered when you take these findings seriously and attempt to incorporate them into change strategies. There are several quality studies of school leadership across different countries that provide consistent and clear, not to say easy, messages (Bryk & Schneider, 2002; Bryk, Sebring, Kerbow, Rollow, & Easton, 1998; Day et al., 2000; James, Connolly, Dunning, & Elliot, 2006; Leithwood, Bauer, & Riedlinger, 2006; Leithwood, Louis, Anderson, & Wahlstrom, 2004; Marzano, Water, & McNulty, 2005; McLaughlin & Talbert, 2001, 2006; Newmann, King, & Youngs, 2000).

Bryk and his colleagues (1998) have been tracing the evolution of reform in Chicago schools since 1988. In schools that evidenced improvement over time (about one-third of 473 elementary schools):

> Principals worked together with a supportive base of parents, teachers, and community members to mobilize initiative. Their efforts broadly focused along two major dimensions: first, reaching out to parents and community to strengthen the ties between local school professionals and the clientele they are to serve; and second, working to expand the professional capaci-ties of individual teachers, to promote the formation of a coher-ent professional community, and to direct resources toward enhancing the quality of instruction. (p. 270)

These successful principals had (1) an "inclusive, facilitative orientation"; (2) an "institutional focus on student learning"; (3) "efficient management"; and (4) "combined pressure and support" (p. 6). They had a strategic orientation, using school improvement plans and instructional focus to "attack incoherence."

> In schools that are improving, teachers are more likely to say that, once a program has begun, there is follow-up to make sure it is working and there is real continuity from one program to

another. In our earlier research, we dubbed schools with high levels of incoherence "Christmas tree schools." Such schools were well-known showcases because of the variety of programs they boasted. Frequently, however, these programs were uncoordinated and perhaps even philosophically inconsistent. (Sebring & Bryk, 2000, pp. 441–442)

In continued work in Chicago, Bryk and Schneider (2002) found that principals are crucial for shaping "trust in schools," which has dramatic influences, both direct and indirect, on the effectiveness of the school. They refer to "the *centrality* of principal leadership" in developing and sustaining relational trust, which establishes the conditions for success (p. 137, emphasis added). They conclude that "only when participants demonstrate their commitment to engage in such work [focused on improvement] and see others doing the same can a genuine professional community grounded in relational trust emerge. [In this respect] principals must take the lead" (p. 139).

Other studies of schools improving are variations on these same themes. The effects of strong and weak professional communities in high schools studied by McLaughlin and Talbert (2001) show that leadership (or lack of it) at the department and/or school level accounted for a large part of these differences:

These very different worlds reveal how much department leadership and expectations shape teacher community. The English department chair actively maintained open department boundaries so that teachers would bring back knowledge resources from districts and out of district professional activities to the community. English faculty attended state and national meetings, published regularly in professional journals, and used professional development days to visit classrooms in other schools. The chair gave priority for time to share each other's writing, discuss new projects, and just talk. English department leadership extended and reinforced expectations and opportunities for teacher learning provided by the district and by the school, developing a rich repertoire of resources for the community to learn.

None of this applied down the hall in the social studies department, where leadership enforced the norms of privatism and conservatism that Dan Lortie found central to school teaching. For example, the Social Studies chair saw department meetings as an irritating ritual rather than an opportunity: "I don't hold meetings once a week; I don't even necessarily have them once a month." Supports or incentives for learning were few in the social studies department. This department chair marginalized the weakest teachers in the department, rather than enabling or encouraging their professional growth. (pp. 107–108)

Only 3 of 16 high schools studied demonstrated school-wide professional communities. In these comparisons, McLaughlin and Talbert talk about "the pivotal role of principal leadership."

The utter absence of principal leadership within Valley High School is a strong frame for the weak teacher community we found across departments in the school; conversely, strong leadership in Greenfield, Prospect and Ibsen has been central to engendering and sustaining these school-wide teacher learning communities. Principals with low scores [on leadership, as perceived by teachers] generally are seen as managers who provide little support or direction for teaching and learning in the school. Principals receiving high ratings are actively involved in the sorts of activities that nurture and sustain strong teacher community. (p. 110)

In their more recent and systematic review of professional learning communities, McLaughlin and Talbert (2006) again tout the principal as central to success. They show that principals are in a strategic position to promote or inhibit the development of a teacher learning community in their schools. They found that effective principals "leverage teacher commitment and support for collaboration," "broker and develop learning resources for teacher communities," and "support transitions between stages of community development" (p. 56). In so doing, principals also spread and develop leaders across the school, thereby creating a critical mass of distributive leadership as a resource for the present and the future.

Day and his colleagues (2000) in England wrote a book on the leadership roles in 12 schools, all of which "had consistently raised student achievement levels—in this sense they were 'improving schools'—and all the head teachers were recognized as being instrumental in this and in the overall success of the schools" (p. 1). We observe a now-familiar refrain:

The vision and practices of these heads were organized around a number of core personal values concerning the modeling and promotion of respect [for individuals], fairness and equality, caring for the well-being and whole development of students and staff, integrity and honesty. (p. 39)

These school leaders were "relationship centered," focused on "professional standards," "outwards looking in" (seeking ideas and connections across the country), and "monitoring school performance." Day and associates conclude,

Within the study, there was also ample evidence that people were trusted to work as powerful professionals, within clear collegial value frameworks, which were common to all. There was a strong emphasis upon teamwork and participation in decision-making (though heads reserved the right to be autocratic). Goals were clear and agreed, communications were good and everyone had high expectations of themselves and others. Those collegial cultures were maintained, however, within contexts of organization and individual accountability set by external policy demands and internal aspirations. These created ongoing tensions and dilemmas, which had to be managed and mediated as part of the establishment and maintenance of effective leadership cultures. (p. 162)

Additional confirmation and clarity are furnished by Newmann and his colleagues (2000), who used the more comprehensive concept of "school capacity," which in turn affects instructional quality and student assessment in the school as a whole. School capacity consists of the collective effectiveness of the whole staff working together to improve student learning for all. Five interrelated components of school capacity were identified.

1. Teachers' knowledge, skills, and dispositions

2. Professional community

3. Program coherence

4. Technical resources

5. Principal leadership

First, professional development related to the knowledge, skills, and dispositions of teachers as individual staff members is a necessary but insufficient element. Obviously, this is important and can make a difference in individual classrooms, but unless connected to collective learning, it fails to influence the culture of the school. Hence, the second factor, which is that there also must be organization development because social or relationship resources are key to school improvement. Thus, schools must combine individual development with the development of *school-wide professional communities.* Individual and collective development need to be twinned if they are to result in increased school capacity.

However, individual development combined with professional communities is still not sufficient unless it is channeled in a way that combats the fragmentation of multiple innovations by working on *program coherence,* "the extent to which the school's programs for student and staff learning are coordinated, focused on clear learning goals, and sustained over a period of time" (Newmann et al., 2000, p. 5). Program coherence is organizational focus and integration. Fourth, instructional improvement requires additional *resources* (materials, equipment, space, time, and access to expertise). Finally, school capacity cannot be developed in the absence of quality leadership. Put differently, *the role of the principal is to cause the previous four factors to get better and better in concert.* Elmore (2004) agrees.

> The job of administrative leaders is primarily about enhancing the skills and knowledge of people in the organization, creating a common culture of expectations around the use of those skills and knowledge, holding the various pieces of the organization together in a productive relationship with each other, and holding individuals accountable for their contributions to the collective result. (p. 15)

James and colleagues (2006) supply an even more compelling and deeply nuanced account of the role of school heads in 12 "very effective primary schools" in Wales. Without exception, say James and colleagues, "they all recognized and articulated the importance of enabling the pupils to learn and of continually improving teaching in the school" (p. 89). These school heads also developed leadership in others, had a modesty about themselves, grasped the big picture, and fostered partnerships with governing bodies, the local authority, and networks beyond the school. The role of leadership, suggest James and colleagues, concerns "those behaviors that enabled others to take up their role in relation to the institution's main and defined task" (p. 97).

My colleague Ken Leithwood has been studying and developing school leadership for four decades. Leithwood, Bauer, and Riedlinger's (2006) current research in New Orleans is an excellent example of testing the limits of the principalship (if there was ever a litmus test for the role of principal under trying conditions, it has to be New Orleans—pre- and/or post-Katrina). Principals were part of a fellows program that supported and cultivated their leadership over time. Leithwood and his colleagues drew 10 lessons from their multiyear study of these principals:

1. Dramatic individual change is possible.

2. One good experience can jump-start a continuous learning ethos.

3. Ongoing support is needed if leaders are to influence student learning.

4. Training should encompass the team as well as the individual principal.

5. Direct, practical help in data-driven decision making is especially critical in the current policy environment.

6. Practice what you preach.

7. A little bit of money goes a long way.

8. For a long-term impact, build a community of leaders.

9. Use the community of leaders to retain successful leaders.

10. Use inspiring leadership models to recruit new leaders.

Leithwood and colleagues stress that a key factor was the availability of opportunities "to continuously discuss and examine programs and practices, to incorporate feedback from fellows, to nurture the network among fellows and otherwise act as steward of the mission" (p. 23).

As part of a major multiyear initiative being conducted under the auspices of the Wallace Foundation, Leithwood and his team (2004) recently analyzed existing research studies in order to determine what we know about "how leadership influences student learning." Not only did they review the research field, they also included a review of reviews, thus consolidating a massive amount of research on the topic. This comprehensive review found that successful leaders engaged in three sets of core practices:

1. Setting directions (shared vision and group goals, high performance expectations)

2. Developing people (individual support, intellectual/emotional stimulation, modeling)

3. Redesigning the organization (collaborative cultures and structures, building productive relations with parents and the community) (p. 4)

Leithwood's group concluded that school leadership accounts for one quarter of the variation on student achievement explained by school-level variables (school-level variables themselves are but a smaller set of other factors, such as family background).

In another thorough review, Marzano, Waters, and McNulty (2005) drew similar conclusions. In *School Leadership That Works,* they examined 69 studies involving 2,802 schools and approximately 1.4 million students and 14,000 teachers. They also found a .25 correlation between the leadership behavior of the principal and student achievement. They identified twenty-one specific behaviors that influence student learning, most of them indirectly (but nonetheless explicitly), through shaping the culture and relationships of people within the school and between the school and the outside.

It should be clear, then, that school improvement is an organizational phenomenon, and therefore the principal, as leader, is the key. With all this confirmation from the research literature and with many current attempts to situate the principal as change leader, one would think that it would be a slam dunk to make progress. Well, it is not, and here is where progress means digging deeper into the problem and its solution.

THE COMPLEXITY OF LEADERSHIP

Let us first examine three cases where the role of the principal was featured as a core part of the change strategy. First, recall the case studies of Chicago, Milwaukee, and Seattle conducted by the Cross City Campaign for Urban School Reform (2005). Money galore and a lot of the seemingly "right" components were incorporated into a district-wide multiyear strategy: a focus on literacy and math, a concentration on assessment for learning data, plenty of professional development, and an emphasis on principals as instructional leaders, with significant accompanying professional development. The end result was limited impact on the classroom. Although they were positioned to play a key role, "principals had multiple responsibilities that often worked at cross purposes with their role of instructional leaders" (p. 9).

With even more prominence, the principalship was central to the delivery of the high-profile, highly supported literacy and math reform in the San Diego City Schools District in the 1997–2002 period (Hubbard, Mehan, & Stein, 2006). The theory of action envisioned principals as "the most critical resource in the professional guidance and instructional direction of school" (p. 75). Called on to be "leaders of instruction," principals were to spend more time in classrooms, engaging teachers in conversations about instruction, and to spend less time on administrative, logistical, and financial matters" (p. 75). Principals also received considerable targeted support, including close working relationships with instructional leaders (a former area superintendent role refashioned to support school improvement). All principals in the district engaged in walk-throughs with their instructional leader, monthly principal conferences where instruction was the only topic, mentorship, support groups, and visits to other schools to observe exemplary practice. In other words, the strategy called for highly detailed and explicit roles for principals as instructional change agents on an ongoing basis. Yet, enormous difficulties were encountered in linking school leadership to instructional improvement across classrooms. I will turn to explanations in a moment, but first one more case.

Supovitz's (2006) case study of Duval County in Florida is equally instructive. Again, this is a case of district-wide, five-year (at this point) reform with a relentless focus on instruction. And once more, principals are recognized as key players, "integral to the spread of instructional reform" (p. 85). Considerable emphasis and support were provided for the professional development of principals for their new role. And again, it did not pan out as envisioned.

What is going on here? Finally, policymakers and district leaders take the research findings on the role of principals seriously, and still hit a wall. In my view, there are three fundamental explanations. First, maybe districts have the strategy wrong. They are expecting principals to carry out roles that are centrally (district) determined. In this case, principals are in the unenviable role of trying to figure out somebody else's strategy. Second, maybe the role as instructional leader is far more daunting than people imagined. Thus, the capacity to be this good requires understanding and skills beyond the preparation and inservice development experiences of most principals. Third, the new expectations have been added to the traditional ones without any consideration of whether the new role in its entirety is feasible under the current working conditions faced by principals.

I favor all three explanations in combination. The net effect is that the principalship is being placed in an impossible position. In short, the changes required to transform cultures are far deeper than we understood; principals do not have the capacity to carry out the new roles; and principals are burdened by too many role responsibilities that inhibit developing and practicing the new competencies—add-ons without anything being taken away. Hard change, low capacity, plenty of distractions—a recipe for frustration. In sum, the principal is key, but we haven't yet figured out how to position the role to fulfill the promise.

This chapter presents a powerful message for school reform. A study found that students who got three good teachers in 3 successive years did much better. Well, students in schools led by principals who foster strong professional communities are much more likely to encounter three good teachers in a row, whether it be on the same day or over the years. The problem is that such schools are in the minority. Definitely unfinished business on the change agenda.

REFERENCES

Bryk, A., & Schneider, B. (2002). *Trust in schools.* New York: Russell Sage.

Bryk, A., Sebring, P. B., Kerbow, D., Rollow, S., & Easton, J. (1998). *Charting Chicago school reform.* Boulder, CO: Westview Press.

Cross City Campaign for Urban School Reform. (2005). *A delicate balance: District policies and classroom practice.* Chicago: Author.

Day, C., Harris, A., Hadfield, M., Toley, H., & Beresford, J. (2000). *Leading schools in times of change.* Buckingham, UK: Open University Press.

Duke, D. L. (1998). Why principals consider quitting. *Phi Delta Kappan, 70*(4), 308–313.

Elmore, R. F. (2004). *School reform from the inside out: Policy, practice, and performance.* Cambridge, MA: Harvard University Press.

Evans, C. (1995, June). Leaders wanted. *Education Week,* p. 1.

Fullan, M. (1997). *What's worth fighting for in the principalship?* (2nd ed.). Toronto: Elementary Teachers Federation of Ontario; New York: Teachers College Press.

Hubbard, L., Mehan, H., & Stein, M. K. (2006). *Reform as learning.* London: Routledge.

James, C., Connolly, M., Dunning, G., & Elliot, T. (2006). *How very effective primary schools work.* London: Paul Chapman.

Leithwood, K., Bauer, S., & Riedlinger, B. (2006). Developing and sustaining school principals. In B. Davies (Ed.), *Sustaining and developing leaders* (pp. 120–145). London: Sage.

Leithwood, K., Louis, K., Anderson, S., & Wahlstrom, K. (2004). *How leadership influences student learning.* New York: Wallace Foundation.

Marzano, R., Waters, T., & McNulty, B. (2005). *School leadership that works.* Alexandria, VA: Association for Supervision and Curriculum Development.

McLaughlin, M., & Talbert, J. (2001). *Professional communities and the work of high school teaching.* Chicago: University of Chicago Press.

McLaughlin, M., & Talbert, J. (2006). *Building school-based teacher learning communities.* New York: Teachers College Press.

Newmann, F., King, B., & Youngs, P. (2000, April). *Professional development that addresses school capacity.* Paper presented at the annual meeting of the American Educational Research Association, New Orleans.

Sammons, P. (1999). *School effectiveness.* Lisse, The Netherlands: Swetz & Zeitlinger.

Sebring, P. B., & Bryk, A. (2000, February). School leadership and the bottom line in Chicago. *Phi Delta Kappan, 81*(6), 440–443.

Supovitz, J. (2006). *The case for district based reform.* Cambridge, MA: Harvard Education Press.

Times Education Supplement. (1997). *TES survey.* London: Author.

CHAPTER SEVEN

Breakthrough Components

Michael Fullan

Peter Hill

Carmel Crévola

A breakthrough will be achieved when virtually all students are served well by the public education system. This can happen only when the pieces required for systemic success are creatively assembled in the service of reform that touches every classroom.

In Senge's (1990) system thinking terms, schools currently have a lot of the needed "inventions," but not enough derivative innovations. Senge states that an invention or a new idea "becomes an innovation only when it can be replicated on a meaningful scale at practical costs" (pp. 5–6). He elaborates:

> When an idea moves from an invention to an innovation, diverse "component technologies" come together. Emerging from isolated developments in separate fields of research, these components gradually form an "ensemble" of technologies that are critical to each other's success . . . . The Wright brothers proved [in 1903] that powered flight was possible, but the McDonnell Douglas DC-3, introduced in 1935, ushered in the era of commercial air travel. The DC-3 was the first plane that supported itself economically as well as aerodynamically. During those intervening thirty years . . . myriad experiments with commercial flight had failed. Like early experiments with learning organizations,

the early plans were not reliable and cost effective on an appropriate scale.

The DC-3, for the first time, brought together five critical component technologies that formed a successful ensemble. They were: the variable pitch propeller, retractable landing gear, a type of lightweight molded body construction . . . radical air-cooled engine, and wing flaps. To succeed, the DC-3 needed all five, four were not enough. (Senge, 1990, p. 6)

Our question, of course, is what are the specific critical components for a breakthrough school system to take off? Before proceeding to answer this question, there is one other powerful metaphor that should guide our efforts. Eric Abrahamson (2004) in *Change Without Pain* (actually change with less pain than usual) compares change strategies that are based on "creative destruction" with those that stem from "creative recombination."

Too often, Abrahamson (2004) says, we start from the assumption that existing systems have little or no value and should be put aside in favor of brand-new solutions. Abrahamson calls this "the creative destruction" strategy, which more specifically results in the *repetitive change* syndrome:

The symptoms? Initiative overload, change-related chaos, and widespread employee anxiety, cynicism, and burnout. The results? Not only do relentless tidal shifts of change create pain at almost every level of the company and make organizational change harder to manage, more costly to implement, and more likely to fail, but they also impinge on routine operations and render firms inwardly focused on managing change rather than outwardly focused on the customers these changes should serve. (Abrahamson, 2004, pp. 2–3)

Examples of repetitive change syndrome in school systems are legion. Although there are some exceptions (and even the positive exceptions, as we have seen, have not yet affected instructional practice), the experiences of the majority of educators are closer to Elmore's (2004) observation:

Local reform initiatives are typically characterized by volatility— jumping nervously from one reform idea to the next over relatively short periods of time—and superficiality—choosing reforms that have little impact on instruction or learning and implementing them in shallow ways. (p. 2)

The neglected and more powerful alternative, argues Abrahamson, is "creative recombination." Change with less pain involves knowing what already exists in the system that can be revised, as well as knowing how you can redeploy and recombine existing elements in the system into new configurations. This, says Abrahamson, "is creative recombination in action" (p. 23).

The answer, then, is closer to home than we think. We have known since the early writings of the father of the study of modern organizations, Peter Drucker, that the failure to exploit existing innovations is more widespread than the failure to innovate in the first place. According to Abrahamson (2004), we are better off to "start with what you have lying around in the corporate [system] basement" (p. 26).

Education reform is at a stage where many of the components of successful large-scale reform are evident in schools' collective basements. One half of the solution is to seek out and identify the critical elements that need to be in place; the other half is combining them creatively. This is not simply a job of alignment but rather one of establishing dynamic connectivity among the core elements.

We start in this chapter by identifying the three critical components that need to be at the core of any breakthrough system.

THE TRIPLE P CORE COMPONENTS

Figure 7.1 displays the three core elements that form our breakthrough system: personalization, precision, and professional learning. In this chapter, we establish their nature and importance, and in subsequent chapters, we provide more operational detail.

Recall Senge's (1990) criteria for innovation to flourish: All three components, not any two, will be required; the costs must be practical; and the benefits must be experienced on a wide scale—in other words, breakthrough criteria. We must also reinforce our previous warning: Any overemphasis on one or two components at the expense of others will be divisive and dysfunctional. The glue that binds these three components is moral purpose: education for all that

Figure 7.1   The Triple P Core Components

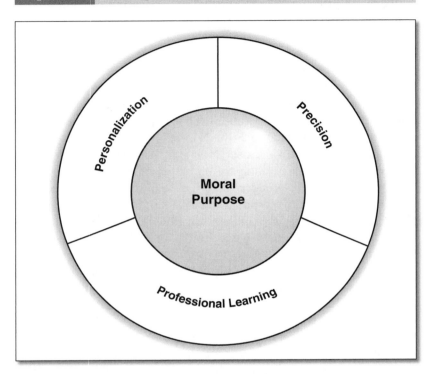

raises the bar as it closes the gap. For this to happen, the three Ps must be synergistically interconnected. When they are, the job becomes easier because each component leverages the others upward.

Personalization

Personalization, or what used to be called *individualization,* is the least advanced in practice of the three core components, although if anything it has a longer history than the other two. In recent years, there has been a renewed interest in personalization, thanks to educators such as Carol Ann Tomlinson (1998), whose work on differentiating classroom instruction has long been a staple resource for teachers and schools striving to implement a more individually tailored instructional program. Breakthrough strives to build on such good work with a meshing of the many components into a streamlined system of operations and processes.

Personalization is education that "puts the learner at the center" (Leadbeater, 2002, p. 1) or, more accurately, puts each and every child at the center and provides an education that is tailored to the students' learning and motivational needs at any given moment. Schools couldn't do this even when only 50% of the population of school-age children was being served, so how will they do it with virtually all children? Yet this is the breakthrough standard we are setting.

Again it has to be practical—less rather than more work for teachers. There are two aspects to personalization: namely, motivation to learn and pedagogical experiences that hit the mark particular for the individual. These aspects are obviously related. Students do not become engaged in learning unless the experience matches or inspires their needs, and exciting learning experiences generate further motivation. It is now well documented that as children go from grade to grade in the educational system their *engagement* with school and learning declines. This is a function of failure to personalize learning (and is related to inadequate linkages to the other two Ps—precision and professional learning).

Imagine a health care worker facing 30 citizens and having the responsibility for helping them establish healthy lifestyles. The health care leader has excellent standards at her disposal. It is clear where everyone should be heading. But the citizens are differently motivated and are at very different starting points. Would inspirational teaching and clear standards carry the day? It would for a few, but not for many. The leader would have to have a way of diagnosing each individual's starting point to sort out where and equally how to proceed initially and every day thereafter. Heifetz and Linsky's (2002) observation about complex adaptive challenges is apt here: "The person with the problem is the problem, and is the solution" (p. 13). This is a personalization statement. Personalization is about individuals, but it is *relational*—between the teacher, the student, the home, and the school.

The mission of the school system is to make personalization a reality. But it must be universal—for all—or it will fail. Personalization is as much a collective as an individual phenomenon.

Aside from the immense practical problem of how to do it, there are dangers if personalization is carried out in the absence of the other components or without the moral purpose of serving all students to a high standard. Personalization often includes choice—by students and by parents. If the capacity to make choices is uneven, greater inequality will occur. Programs involving school choice within public systems, let alone systems that provide public funds to choose private educational options, are divisive and would not meet our breakthrough criteria.

Instead, our view is that every public school and every teacher (individually and collectively) should be skilled at personalizing learning—putting the individual student (each one) at the center of learning. If this happens, the divisive tendencies to choose alternative schools will dissipate or otherwise operate within acceptable bounds of a system that is good for all. So, the first challenge for the new mission of schools is how to make personalization of learning for everyone a practical reality. In the absence of pervasive personalization, the opposite will happen— mass production, a one-size-fits-all mentality that serves only those who benefit from the status quo.

Precision

To be *precise* is to get something right; to *prescribe* is to lay down rigid rules. Precision is in the service of personalization because it means to be uniquely accurate, that is, precise to the learning needs of the individual. Here, a great deal of progress has been made recently in education's corporate basement under the practice of "assessment for learning" (using data as a tool for improving teaching and learning); there remains one fatal weakness—how to go from assessment to improvement of instructional practice in the classroom (again, for each and every child). Schools need to get assessment for learning out of the basement, clean it up, and creatively recombine it with personalization and continuous professional learning.

Remarkably, the theory of assessment for learning was laid out in clear and comprehensive terms many years ago by a number of writers. For example, 15 years ago, Sadler (1989) developed answers to two problems: (1) the lack of a theory of feedback and formative assessment in complex learning settings and (2) the puzzling observation that even when teachers provide students with valid and reliable judgments about the quality of their work, improvement does not necessarily follow (p. 119).

Sadler's main solution, way ahead of its time, was to focus on "how judgments about the quality of student responses (performances, pieces, or works) can be used to shape and improve the student's competence by short-circuiting the randomness and inefficiency of trial and error learning" (p. 120). Consistent with our solution, Sadler said that *feedback* is the key element of formative assessment, but feedback qualifies as feedback *"only when it is used to alter the gap"* of learning (Sadler's italics, p. 121). Stated explicitly, Sadler observed,

> The learner has to (a) possess a concept of the *standard* (or goal, or reference level) being aimed for, (b) compare the *actual* (or current) *level of performance* with the standard, and (c) engage in appropriate *action* which leads to some closure of the gap. (p. 121, italics in original)

Sadler argued,

> Qualitative [personalized] judgments are invariably involved in appraising a student's performance. In such learnings, student development is multidimensional rather than sequential, and pre-requisite learning cannot be conceptualized as neatly packaged units of skills or knowledge. Growth takes place on many interrelated fronts at once and is continuous rather than lock-step. (p. 123)

For a system of continuous learning to work, standards must be communicated and be available to students. In a teaching setting, this presupposes that the teacher already possesses the knowledge of what is expected for given learners. However, "teachers' conceptions of quality are typically held largely in unarticulated form, inside their heads as tacit knowledge" (Sadler, 1989, p. 126). Such knowledge

> keeps the concept of the standard relatively inaccessible to the learner, and tends to maintain the learner's dependence on the teacher for judgments about the quality of performance. How to draw the concept of excellence out of the heads of teachers, give it some external formulation, and make it available to the learner, is a non-trivial problem. (Sadler, 1989, p. 127)

Not to mention the fact that some teachers' tacit knowledge may be vague or erroneous.

Feedback is at the heart of what is known as *assessment for learning*—a high-yield strategy of improvement that has come on the scene strongly in the past five years. The work of Black and

Wiliam (1998a; 1998b) and Stiggins (2004) attests to the power and prominence of assessment for learning as a core precision-based component of reform.

As they do with most potentially high-yield solutions, systems have gone overboard on assessment as a solution. Systems have swamped schools with assessments and standards to the detriment of manageable and precise action. Too much of a good thing is a bad thing. Precision means refinement, not death by information overdose. Not only must feedback be relative to standards and performance, but assessment for learning must also provide feedback to the teacher about *instruction* so that he or she can construct the instructional focus and set the goals of the lesson accordingly. Feedback, in other words, can be taken to extremes if it provides mounds of undigested information or if it is taken to imply impossible tasks for teachers, such as having to organize individual conferences with students every day.

We see the glut of information in well-intentioned systemwide reform initiatives in Chicago, Milwaukee, and Seattle (Cross City Campaign, 2005). In those results-oriented districts, information on test scores was ubiquitous. The problem that we tackle in breakthrough is not only how to make data more manageable but also precisely *how to link data to instruction on a daily basis*— something that so far has evaded even the most results-oriented districts. And, we must do so without falling into the prescription trap of fostering student dependency. We must recognize that data-driven instruction is a strategy for improving pedagogy as a more precise causal link to student learning.

Breakthrough is intended to set the stage for classroom instruction in which the current sporadic data collection is streamlined, analysis is automated, and individualized instruction is delivered on a *daily* basis in *every* classroom. Now that is revolutionary.

Breakthrough represents a beginning for those who are nowhere near using data for improvement. For those who are down the track (and there are increasing numbers, thanks to the likes of Black and Wiliam, Stiggins, and developers of new approaches to using data, such as Good and Kaminski, 2002), breakthrough is a call to take the next step in achieving greater precision in classroom instruction.

In our experience, even those who think they are well into assessment for learning soon realize that they have a way to go. Even in the best districts in this regard, the expertise lies in the hands of a few. The rhetoric of assessment for learning is abundant, but the knowledge in reality is very thin on the ground. The missing piece in most cases is a manageable system for going from data to instruction.

Breakthrough is about linking all the core pieces of the puzzle—within assessment for learning, in this case—and across the three core Ps of personalization, precision, and professional learning. Without our framework, educators often have many of the pieces, but they come from different puzzles. No wonder people cannot make a picture!

Educators have assessments, but they are often selected from bits of this and that, small pieces of the whole. Increasingly, teachers are helped in analyzing the data, receiving feedback in terms of scores, and sometimes even skill analysis. The missing step and next piece is to make sense of the whole thing as *one unified picture* of where each student lies in terms of where to go next. For this, teachers need a manageable ongoing monitoring process that feeds into their knowledge for informing instruction.

Speaking of puzzle pieces, the systems we are talking about do not imply individual teachers would be doing these things, *but* collectivities of teachers. Elmore (2004), as we noted earlier, stresses that you cannot have effective external accountability in the absence of a capacity for internal (to the school) accountability. The most effective schools combine (1) individual responsibility and (2) collective expectations in a system that (3) aligns responsibility, expectation, and accountability, and that (4) incorporates external accountability demands (Elmore, p. 141).

Elmore found that:

> In these schools, collective expectations gelled into highly inter-active, relatively coherent, informal and formal systems, by which teachers and administrators held each other accountable for their actions vis-à-vis students. Teachers and administrators in this category of school were able to describe and interpret the formal external accountability systems in which their schools operated (such as testing systems, curriculum guidelines . . .) but in no case did those external systems seem to exercise the determining influence over their individual conceptions of responsibility, their collective expectations of each other or their students. (p. 193)

We are now approaching the third piece of our unified puzzle—the learning of teachers individually and as a group. Personalization requires precision, and precision demands ongoing learning.

Professional Learning

We have deliberately selected the term *professional learning* over the more narrow conceptual terms of *professional development* or *professional learning communities* because breakthrough means focused, ongoing learning for each and every teacher.

You can't have personalization and precision without daily learning on the part of teachers, both individually and collectively. Over the past decade, education's hypothetical corporate basement (Abrahamson, 2004) has become cluttered with valuable bits and pieces of how teachers can best learn. It is time for some creative recombinations in the service of focused instruction.

In a detailed study of mathematics reform in California, Cohen and Hill (2001) argue that ongoing teacher learning is the key to linking new conceptions of instructional practice with assessment of student learning. They comment that the policy was intended to create coherence among elements of curriculum, assessment, and learning opportunities for teachers. But,

> Such coherence is quite rare in the blizzard of often divergent professional development that typically blows over U.S. public schools. Only a modest fraction of California elementary teachers—roughly 10 percent—had these experiences. Standards, assessments, and accountability are more likely to succeed if they are accompanied by extended opportunities for professional learning that are grounded in practice. (pp. 9–10)

Over the past decade, it has become a given that any major reform initiative must be accompanied by investments in professional development. Breakthrough is about how to refine and focus these investments in a way that will yield predictable continuous benefits for teachers and students.

The system is making progress, but not nearly enough as we saw from Cohen and Hill (2001; only 1 in 10 teachers evidenced significant learning, with no indication that the positive learning experiences would continue for the fortunate 10%). Confirmation of limited impact despite major focus and resources comes from Borman and Associates' (2005) investigation of mathematics and science reform in Chicago, El Paso, Memphis, and Miami.

Each city was the recipient of $15 million from the National Science Foundation's (NSF) Urban Systemic Initiative. Again, the strategy seemed to have all the right elements: a curriculum focus, a systemic orientation, plenty of investment in professional development, and an advanced conception of math and science learning. The policy and curriculum documents stated, "instruction should emphasize active learning and high order thinking skills while providing investigative and problem-solving opportunities for all students" (Borman and Associates, 2005, p. 4).

NSF's "Six Drivers Model" appears unassailable:

1. Implementation of a comprehensive, standards-based curriculum

2. Development of a coherent, consistent set of policies that support broad-based reform

3. Convergence of all resources that are designed to support the reform

4. Broad-based support from parents, policymakers, institutions of higher education, business and industry, foundations

5. Accumulation of a broad and deep array of evidence that the program does affect student achievement positively

6. Improving the achievement of all students, including those historically underserved

In reality, Borman and her colleagues (2005) found "only tenuous links between professional development and classroom instruction for many teachers. Most teachers seemed to experience a disconnection between their professional development experiences and their day-to-day classroom experiences" (pp. 70–71).

Borman and colleagues also found that despite professional development sessions, which were based on extensive modeling of the new pedagogy focusing on specific instructional practices with students as active learners, little change in classrooms ensued. In their overall sample, they found through classroom observation that 78% of teaching remained teacher centered (didactic), 16% was subject centered, and less than 6% was student centered (p. 98).

Correspondingly, in evaluating classroom practices from the students' perspective (through observation and focused group interviews), Borman and colleagues found limited student engagement in learning:

> Based upon our results, if we consider the amount of class time during which students have opportunities to learn new concepts and acquire new skills, we are left with the unhappy reality that current professional development activities are not translating into the classroom with effective instructional strategies and content. (p. 153)

Recall that this limited impact occurred despite the fact that "both district and school administrators viewed the provision of professional development opportunities as a primary focus for reform implementation" (Borman & Associates, 2005, p. 216). Thus, educators appreciate that professional development is a sine qua non of success but have not converted this commitment into a high-yield strategy.

We can return to the larger Cross City Campaign (2005) evaluation of reforms in Chicago, Milwaukee, and Seattle to confirm that professional development is a central strategy but one that is problematic to implement effectively at the classroom and school levels.

Cross City Campaign (2005, p. 9) researchers found that most teachers experienced professional development as fragmented and not linked to their classroom practice, although districts were making some progress in improving the quality of individual sessions. In Seattle, for example, "professional development was a major tool for implementing reform"—one of the three key strategic standards (the other two are "Standards-Based Reform" and "Transformational Academic Planning Process"). As the researchers conclude, "the strength of the individual professional development offerings was sometimes quite high, but there was no overarching umbrella to integrate them. As one administrator observed, 'the ideas are good ideas and well intentioned. There's just no follow through'" (p. 80).

So, what's the solution? Generally, it involves turning the problem on its head. The solution does not involve attempting to coordinate centrally driven professional development, which (1) usually doesn't work or (2) can yield results only by resorting to behavioristic prescription, which we maintain is self-defeating.

Instead, schools need to work from the classroom outward—and glimpses of this solution are seen in the large-scale studies we just reviewed. Professional development works when it is "school-based and embedded in teachers' daily work" (Cross City Campaign, 2005, p. 10). And Cohen and Hill (2001) show that new policies and resources provide the potential for "new opportunities to learn, rooted either in improved student curriculum or in examples of students' work on assessments, or both" (p. 9).

The problem is that these grounded learning opportunities, even in situations with great system presence, are experienced by only a small minority of teachers (10 to 20%), and in all likelihood, these teachers are in the best circumstances. The kind of professional learning we are talking about in this book is available only for a minority of teachers and, even in those best-case scenarios, is not likely to be sustained for those teachers. This is why we are proposing a system change.

Let's be clear. We are not saying that only 10 to 20% of teachers are learning. Teachers learn every day. And most of them these days are learning to move literacy and math scores upward. What we are saying is that the conditions for learning for the vast majority of teachers are not conducive to the breakthrough we need to fulfill the new mission of schools.

How, then, do we make deeper daily learning a reality for teachers? Replacing the concept of professional development with professional learning is a good start; understanding that professional learning "in context" is the only learning that changes classroom instruction is a second step. Elmore (2004) got it right: "Improvement is more a function of *learning to do the right things* in the setting where you work" (p. 73).

We would have also italicized "in the setting where you work." Elmore elaborates on this fundamental insight:

> The problem [is that] there is almost no opportunity for teachers to engage in continuous and sustained learning about their practice in the setting in which they actually work, observing and being observed by their colleagues in their own classrooms and classrooms of other teachers in other schools confronting similar problems of practice. (p. 127)

It is not just a matter of teachers interacting; they must do so in relation to focused instruction. Professional learning communities can contribute mightily to altering school conditions, but by themselves, they do not go deep enough into classroom practice, and they can even be (unwittingly) counterproductive if their interactions reinforce teaching practices that are ineffective (Cohen & Hill, 2001).

Our reluctant conclusion is that the most ambitious reforms have fallen miserably short of establishing the new mission of schools where virtually all students are engaged in their own significant learning. We need to start at the classroom, reconstructing the problem and the solution as one of embedding personalization, precision, and teacher learning into the daily experiences of students and educators. In so doing, we need to build an infrastructure that surrounds the classroom and will make such transformation inevitable. Moreover, it must be practically achievable.

Education for all can be attained only by transforming the last frontier of educational reform, classroom instruction, and this in turn requires a focus on using data to make instruction more precise. It will also require breakthrough leadership across the infrastructure.

There will be much more to be done. Our goal is to make the case morally and intellectually clear and compelling. Despite failed reform efforts that have given us glimpses of a positive future—and perhaps arising from those efforts—we believe that we could be on the brink of a radical breakthrough. It is time to make learning an exciting and deeply rewarding enterprise for all.

REFERENCES

Abrahamson, E. (2004). *Change without pain.* Boston: Harvard Business School Press.

Black, P., & Wiliam, D. (1998a). Assessment and classroom learning. *Assessment in Education, 5*(1), 7–74.

Black, P., & Wiliam, D. (1998b, October). Inside the black box: Raising standards through classroom assessment. *Phi Delta Kappan, 80*(2), 139–148.

Borman, K., & Associates (2005). *Meaningful urban education reform: Confronting the learning crisis in mathematics and science.* Albany: State University of New York Press.

Cohen, D., & Hill, H. (2001). *Learning policy.* New Haven, CT: Yale University Press.

Cross City Campaign for Urban School Reform. (2005). *A delicate balance: District policies and classroom practice.* Chicago: Author.

Elmore, R. F. (2004). *School reform from the inside out: Policy, practice, and performance.* Cambridge, MA: Harvard University Press.

Good, R. H., & Kaminski, R. A. (Eds.). (2002). *Dynamic indicators of basic early literacy skills* (6th ed.). Eugene, OR: Institute for the Development of Educational Achievement.

Heifetz, R., & Linsky, M. (2002). *Leadership on the line.* Boston: Harvard Business School Press.

Leadbeater, C. (2002). *Learning about personalization.* London: Innovation Unit, Department for Education and Skills.

Sadler, D. R. (1989). Formative assessment in the design of instructional systems. *Instructional Science, 18,* 119–144.

Senge, P. (1990). *The fifth discipline.* New York: Doubleday.

Stiggins, R. (2004). New assessment beliefs for a new school mission. *Phi Delta Kappan, 86*(1), 22–27.

Tomlinson, C. A. (1998). *The differentiated classroom: Responding to the needs of all learners.* Alexandria, VA: Association for Supervision and Curriculum Development.

CHAPTER EIGHT

New Insights Into Professional Learning Communities at Work

Rick DuFour

Rebecca DuFour

Bob Eaker

> *Strong professional learning communities produce schools that are engines of hope and achievement for students. . . . There is nothing more important for education in the decades ahead than educating and supporting leaders in the commitments, understandings, and skills necessary to grow such schools where a focus on effort-based ability is the norm.*
>
> —Jonathon Saphier

> *New knowledge is the most valuable commodity on earth. The more truth we have to work with, the richer we become.*
>
> —Kurt Vonnegut

According to legend, when good friends Ralph Waldo Emerson and Henry David Thoreau reunited after a long separation, each would ask his colleague, "What has become clearer to you since last we met?" It has now been 10 years since we wrote *Professional Learning Communities at Work: Best Practices for Enhancing Student Achievement* (DuFour & Eaker, 1998). In this volume, *Revisiting Professional Learning Communities at Work,* we answer the question, "What has become more clear to us regarding the promise, potential, problems, and pitfalls surrounding the professional learning community (PLC) concept?"

Our conviction regarding the vital role the PLC concept plays in school improvement has only grown over the years. Professional organizations and researchers echo that conviction, and they now routinely call upon educators to organize schools and districts into PLCs to improve both student and adult learning. In fact, the term *professional learning community,* which prior to 1998 was used primarily among educational researchers, has now become part of the routine jargon of educators throughout North America. The term is now used so ubiquitously to describe any loose grouping of educators that it is in danger of losing all meaning.

While the term *professional learning community* has become commonplace, the actual practices of a PLC have yet to become the norm in education. Too many schools, districts, and organizations calling themselves PLCs do virtually none of the things that characterize PLCs. Despite the increasing popularity of the term, actually transforming the culture of a traditional school to reflect the PLC concept remains a complex and challenging task. We are convinced educators would benefit from both greater clarity regarding the PLC concept and specific strategies for implementing the concept. We hope this book will provide both.

WHAT IS A PROFESSIONAL LEARNING COMMUNITY?

We define a professional learning community as *educators committed to working collaboratively in ongoing processes of collective inquiry and action research to achieve better results for the students they serve. Professional learning communities operate under the assumption that the key to improved learning for students is continuous, job-embedded learning for educators* (DuFour, DuFour, Eaker, & Many, 2006).

In *Professional Learning Communities at Work* (1998), we identified six characteristics of PLCs, and in *Learning by Doing* (2006), we delved into those characteristics in more detail:

1. Shared Mission (Purpose), Vision (Clear Direction), Values (Collective Commitments), and Goals (Indicators, Timelines, and Targets)—All Focused on Student Learning

The very essence of a *learning* community is a focus on and a commitment to the learning of each student. When a school or district functions as a PLC, educators embrace high levels of learning for all students as both the reason the organization exists and the fundamental responsibility of those who work within it. To achieve this shared purpose, the members of a PLC create and are guided by a clear and compelling vision of what their schools and districts must become to help all students learn. They make collective commitments that clarify what each member will do to contribute to creating such organizations, and they use results-oriented goals to mark their progress. This foundation of shared mission (purpose), vision (clear direction), values (collective commitments), and goals (indicators, timelines, and targets) not only addresses *how* educators will work to improve their schools, but also reinforces the moral purpose and collective responsibility that clarify *why* their day-to-day work is so important.

2. A Collaborative Culture With a Focus on Learning

If shared purpose, vision, collective commitments, and goals constitute the foundation of a PLC, then the collaborative team is the fundamental building block of the organization. A PLC is composed of collaborative teams whose members work *interdependently* to achieve *common goals*—goals linked to the purpose of learning for all—for which members are held *mutually accountable*. It is difficult to overstate the importance of collaborative teams in the PLC process. It is equally important, however, to emphasize that collaboration does not lead to improved results unless people are focused on the right issues. Collaboration is a means to an end, not the end itself. In many schools, staff members are willing to collaborate on a variety of topics as long as the focus of the conversation stops at their classroom door. In a PLC, *collaboration* is a systematic process in which teachers work together, interdependently, to analyze and *impact* professional practice in order to improve results for their students, their team, and their school.

3. Collective Inquiry Into Best Practice and Current Reality

Educators in a PLC engage in collective inquiry into (1) best practices about teaching and learning, (2) a candid clarification of their current practices, and (3) an honest assessment of their students' current levels of learning. Collective inquiry helps educators build shared knowledge, which, in turn, allows them to make more informed (and therefore better) decisions and increases the likelihood they will arrive at consensus. Educators in a PLC have an acute sense of curiosity and openness to new possibilities.

4. Action Orientation: Learning by Doing

Members of PLCs are action oriented: They move quickly to turn aspirations into action and visions into reality. They understand that the most powerful learning always occurs in a context of taking action, and they value engagement and experience as the most effective teachers. In fact, the very reason that teachers work together in teams and engage in collective inquiry is to serve as catalysts for action. Learning by doing develops a deeper and more profound knowledge and greater commitment than learning by reading, listening, planning, or thinking (Pfeffer & Sutton, 2000). Furthermore, educators in PLCs recognize that until members of the organization "do" differently, there is no reason to anticipate different results. They avoid paralysis by analysis and overcome inertia with action.

5. A Commitment to Continuous Improvement

Persistent disquiet with the status quo and a constant search for a better way to achieve goals and accomplish the purpose of the organization are inherent in the PLC culture. Systematic processes engage each member of the organization in an ongoing cycle of

- Gathering evidence of current levels of student learning
- Developing strategies and ideas to build on strengths and address weaknesses in that learning
- Implementing the strategies and ideas
- Analyzing the impact of the changes to discover what was effective and what was not
- Applying the new knowledge in the next cycle of continuous improvement

The goal is not simply learning a new strategy but rather creating conditions for perpetual learning. This creates an environment in which innovation and experimentation are viewed not as tasks to be accomplished or projects to be completed but as ways of conducting day-to-day business—forever. Furthermore, participation in this process is not reserved for those designated as leaders; instead, it is a responsibility of every member of the organization.

6. Results Orientation

Finally, members of a PLC realize that all of their efforts in these areas—a focus on learning, collaborative teams, collective inquiry, action orientation, and continuous improvement—must be assessed on the basis of results rather than intentions. Unless initiatives are subjected to ongoing assessment on the basis of tangible results, they represent random groping in the dark, not purposeful improvement. As Peter Senge and Fred Kofman (1995) have concluded, "The rationale for any strategy for building a learning organization revolves around the premise that such organizations will produce dramatically improved results" (p. 44).

THE BIG IDEAS THAT DRIVE PROFESSIONAL LEARNING COMMUNITIES

Noel Tichy (1997) contends that great leaders are able to translate the purpose and priorities of their organizations into a few big ideas that unite people and give them a sense of direction in their day-to-day work. We have found it helpful to frame the PLC concept within three big ideas.

First, the fundamental purpose of the school is to ensure all students learn at high levels, and the future success of students will depend on how effective educators are in achieving that fundamental purpose. There must be no ambiguity or hedging regarding this commitment to learning, and schools must align all practices, procedures, and policies in light of that fundamental purpose. Members of a PLC work together to clarify exactly what each student must learn, monitor each students' learning on a timely basis, provide systematic interventions that ensure students receive additional time and support for learning when they struggle, and extend and enrich learning when students have already mastered the intended outcomes. A corollary assumption stipulates that if all students are to learn at high levels, the adults in the organization must also be continually learning. Therefore structures are created to ensure staff members engage in job-embedded learning as part of their routine work practices.

Second, schools cannot achieve the fundamental purpose of learning for all if educators work in isolation. Therefore school administrators and teachers must build a collaborative culture in which they work together interdependently and assume collective responsibility for the learning of all students.

Third, schools will not know whether or not all students are learning unless educators are hungry for evidence that students are acquiring the knowledge, skills, and dispositions deemed most essential to their success. Schools must systematically monitor student learning on an ongoing basis and use evidence of results to respond immediately to students who experience difficulty, to inform individual and collective practice, and to fuel continuous improvement.

PURPOSEFUL LANGUAGE

As we were determining the title for *Professional Learning Communities at Work,* we chose each word of that title very purposefully. A *professional* is someone with expertise in a specialized field, an individual who has not only pursued advanced training to enter the field but who is also expected to remain current in its evolving knowledge base. The knowledge base of education has expanded dramatically in the past 30 years, both in terms of research and in the articulation of recommended standards for the profession. Educators in a *professional* learning community make these findings the basis of their collaborative investigation into how they can better achieve their goals. They *practice* teaching and leading by constantly enhancing their skills and knowledge in the same way a doctor practices medicine or a lawyer practices law.

The term *learning* also carries significant weight in the title. One of the major challenges in the implementation of the PLC concept is convincing educators to shift from a focus on teaching to a focus on learning—to move beyond the question "Was it taught?" to the far more relevant question "Was it learned?" We advocate for *learning* communities, not *teaching* communities, and argue that the best way to improve student learning is to invest in the learning of the adults who serve them.

Learning suggests ongoing action and perpetual curiosity. In Chinese, the term *learning* is represented by two characters: The first means "to study," and the second means "to practice constantly." The only hope for creating schools and districts that are continuously improving upon their capacity to raise student achievement is to establish the expectation that educators must engage in the ongoing study and constant practice of their field. If all students are to learn, those who educate them must be lifelong learners.

Much had been written about learning organizations when we wrote our original book, but we have always preferred the term *community*. While the term *organization* evokes images of structure and efficiency, the term *community* suggests a group linked by common interests. As Thomas Sergiovanni (2005) writes, "Communities spring from common understandings that provide members with a sense of identity, belonging, and involvement that results in a web of meaningful relationships with moral overtones" (p. 55). Communities form around common characteristics, experiences, practices, or beliefs that are important enough to bind members to one another in a kind of fellowship (Carey & Frohnen, 1998). Successful communities provide members with broadly shared opportunities to participate, promote collective responsibility, and foster a strong sense of belonging (Clinton, 2007).

In a professional learning *community* all of these characteristics are evident. Educators create an environment that fosters shared understanding, a sense of identity, high levels of involvement, mutual cooperation, collective responsibility, emotional support, and a strong sense of belonging as they work together to achieve what they cannot accomplish alone.

WHAT HAS BECOME MORE CLEAR?

In the time since we wrote *Professional Learning Communities at Work,* we have acquired much knowledge as we have worked with schools and districts to implement the PLC concept. This enables us to offer richer and more helpful ideas to contemporary educators. In short, much has become more clear to us about improving learning both for students and adults. Therefore this book will not only review the core concepts and practices of a PLC, it will also explore each of the following 12 new and/or deeper learnings in detail:

1. The Necessity (and Challenge) of Shaping the Culture of the School and District

Educators who cultivate PLCs must engage in an intentional process to impact the culture of their schools and districts. When they are successful, their organizations will undergo profound cultural shifts. We certainly stressed the importance of culture—*the assumptions, beliefs, values, expectations, and habits that constitute the norm for an organization*—in *Professional Learning Communities at Work.* What has become more clear to us is that those who hope to reculture a school district will face two very significant barriers. First, educators have been conditioned to regard school improvement as programs to adopt practices to implement rather than as an ongoing process to build their collective capacity to achieve the purpose, priorities, and goals of their organizations. It is not unusual for us to hear a faculty say, "We do PLCs on Thursday mornings"—a telltale sign they have missed the central premise of the PLC concept and have simply added a new practice to their existing school culture. When the culture has truly shifted, a faculty recognizes that they *are* a PLC; they do not *do* PLCs. They subject every practice, program, policy, and procedure to ongoing review and constant evaluation according to very different assumptions than those that guided the school in the past.

The second barrier to reculturing is particularly formidable. Diarist Anaïs Nin observed, "We don't see things as they are, we see things as we are." Every one of us develops patterns of thought or mental models that represent complex webs of our ideas and assumptions about the world in which we live (Senge, 1990). These models filter our observations and experiences and help us make sense of them. New information gets processed to conform to the ongoing stories we tell ourselves. Anything inconsistent with that story or contrary to our mental models is likely to be dismissed or ignored. "People," Emerson wrote, "only see what they are prepared to see."

Organizational theorists advise that a key to improving any organization is honestly assessing the current reality (Collins, 2001) and confronting the hard facts (Pfeffer & Sutton, 2006). Who could oppose such sound advice? We have discovered, however, that the problem in improving schools is not presenting compelling evidence of the need for change, or even demonstrating the most promising strategies for raising student achievement; the problem is that the evidence and strategies often get filtered through the mental models and mythology of the hard-working, well-intentioned educators who are ultimately called upon to do differently.

The case for operating schools and districts as PLCs is compelling; it is supported by research, proved in practice, endorsed by professional organizations, and best of all, grounded in common sense. We cannot recall a single time when we have reviewed the evidence in support of PLCs with a group of educators, and they then opposed the concept. No staff has ever argued schools are more effective when teachers work in isolation, when they focus on what is taught rather than on what is learned, when high-stakes summative assessments are the only tools used to monitor student learning, or when the response to students who are not learning is left to the discretion of each teacher. But later, all too often, the existing mental models and prevailing mythology begin to erode and distort the PLC concept. Examples of the prevailing mythology include the following:

- "Not all kids can be expected to learn at high levels, because learning is a function of ability, and ability is distributed along the bell-shaped curve."
- "It is my job to teach and their job to learn."

- "We won't be able to improve student learning until parents, the administration, the school board, the legislature, and society do a better job of fulfilling their responsibilities."
- "The schedule won't let us."
- "If we give students additional opportunities to learn when they struggle, we teach them to be irresponsible and deprive them of the important lessons to be learned through failure."
- "I am the king of my kingdom, and as a professional, I want the autonomy to make my own decisions unencumbered from the opinions of others in my school."
- "As a teacher, I am only responsible for the students in my classroom, and I do not intend to take on responsibility for other students or have others interfere in my work with my students."
- "As a principal, I am only responsible for what goes on in my own school, and I don't want to take on responsibility for helping to improve other schools."
- "We are working as hard as humanly possible, and everything we are currently doing is vital, so we cannot stop doing anything we are doing or add any more to our already full plates."
- "You can find research to support anything, and researchers do not understand the world of practitioners, so we should not be persuaded by research."
- "People can skew data to say anything they want, so we should not be persuaded by data."
- "I have always done it this way, and I have been successful."
- "It is the administration's job to improve the school, not mine."
- "If we just had more resources, all our problems would be solved."
- "We cannot go forward unless everyone agrees, because you cannot insist that people do something they do not choose to do."
- "I have worked hard to create 'my stuff' for my class, and I do not want to share my materials with others."
- "This is just the latest fad, and it too shall pass."
- "I have too much content to cover to take the time to gather evidence that students are learning."
- "We are doing as well or better than the schools around us, and the parents seem satisfied, so it would be foolish to tinker with success."
- "Teachers do not have the expertise to develop good curriculum, write valid assessments, or analyze data, so this work should be left to the experts."

The words President John F. Kennedy spoke at Yale University in 1962 are uncannily appropriate when applied to the world of public education:

> As every past generation has had to disenthrall itself from an inheritance of truisms and stereotypes, so in our own time we must move on from the reassuring repetition of stale phrases to a new, difficult, but essential confrontation with reality. For the great enemy of truth is very often not the lie—deliberate, contrived, and dishonest—but the myth—persistent, persuasive, and unrealistic. . . . Mythology distracts us everywhere.

There is no easy way to overcome the obstacle of mythology when engaged in school improvement. It involves making thinking explicit and calling upon people to engage in the difficult task of articulating and examining their assumptions. It calls for building shared knowledge and learning by doing. It requires breaking free of inertia by creating new experiences for people that call upon them to act in new ways. It demands constant and consistent commitment to a sustained direction during an extended period of time. There is no one "A-ha!" moment when the existing culture will give way to new assumptions, beliefs, values, expectations, and habits that constitute the norm for the school or district. The transformation requires fierce resolve, tremendous passion, and relentless persistence. No matter how effectively the case is made for building the capacity of a staff to function as a PLC, much work will remain to be done.

2. The Tendency for Hard Facts About School Improvement to Be Distorted Into Dangerous Half-Truths

Stanford University researchers Jeffrey Pfeffer and Robert Sutton (2006) have concluded organizations often distort clear and compelling evidence of best practice into dangerous half-truths. We have repeatedly seen this phenomenon at work in schools and districts throughout North America. The existing mythology of schooling is so seductive that rather than recognizing the need to create a new culture based on new assumptions, educators are prone to adopt and dilute ideas and concepts to fit their existing culture. They opt for "sorta PLCs," and the concept begins a slow but inevitable death from the constant compromises of its core principles. We will identify examples of how powerful, hard facts are being distorted into dangerous half-truths in education.

3. The Importance of an
Action Orientation, or "Learning by Doing"

In *Professional Learning Communities at Work,* we stressed the importance of building the foundation of a PLC through the articulation of shared mission (purpose), vision (clear direction), values (collective commitments), and goals (indicators, timelines, and targets). We offered strategies and templates for leading the dialogue and generating the documents designed to reflect this solid foundation for moving forward. It has become apparent, however, that schools and districts often settle for merely creating documents rather than implementing ideas. In many instances, little is done to align organizational practices or individual actions with the expressed purpose and priorities. We have come to understand that writing a mission statement has often been used as a substitute for living a mission. Dialogue and documents can be used to create the illusion of change and to impede rather than promote meaningful action. Therefore it is important to repeatedly return to the questions, "What would it look like if we really meant what we said?" and "What specific actions can we expect to see in light of our priorities?"

4. The Importance of Frequent
Common Formative Assessments

In *Professional Learning Communities at Work,* we listed two questions to guide the work of a PLC: "What is it we want our students to learn?" and "How will we respond when they do not learn?" Later in the book, we discussed teachers developing common assessments as part of their collaborative team process. We implied that teachers would work together to answer the question, "How will we know if our students are learning?" But, in retrospect, we did not give this issue nearly enough attention. We have come to understand that one of the most powerful strategies available to a school that hopes to become an effective PLC is to engage teachers in the creation of high-quality common assessments. The question, "How do we know if our students are acquiring the intended knowledge, skills, and dispositions of this course, grade level, or unit of instruction?" is the linchpin of the PLC process and a critical component of the work of collaborative teams. Furthermore, the work of Doug Reeves, Dylan Wiliam, Paul Black, Rick Stiggins, and others has helped us come to a much deeper appreciation of the importance and power of *formative* assessments, assessments used as part of the teaching and learning process instead of assessments administered only to provide a grade.

5. The Importance of Providing Teachers With Relevant and Timely Information (Not Data) as a Catalyst for Improving Teaching

We have concluded schools and teachers suffer from the DRIP syndrome: They are data rich, but information poor. Most teachers are awash in data, but data alone will neither inform nor improve a teacher's practice, and students will not achieve at higher levels unless teachers are becoming more effective in their classrooms. Without relevant information on their respective strengths and weaknesses, teacher conversations regarding the most effective ways to help students learn a concept will deteriorate into sharing of uninformed opinions—"This is how I like to teach it." Improving teacher practice requires informed and precise conversation about effective techniques, and the best way to provide teachers with the tools for that conversation is to ensure each receives frequent and timely information regarding the achievement of his or her students in reaching an agreed-upon standard on a valid assessment in comparison to other similar students attempting to achieve the same standard.

6. The Importance of a Systematic Response When Students Don't Learn, and a Process for Enriching and Expanding Learning When Students Are Already Proficient

In *Professional Learning Communities at Work,* we made repeated references to the significance of a collective response when students did not learn. We did not, however, adequately address what such a response would look like in the real world of schools. We attempt to address that here by providing parameters for and examples of systematic interventions that ensure students receive additional time and support for learning when they struggle. We have also asked educators to tackle the issue of how schools can expand and enrich learning for students who are already proficient in the skills being taught.

7. The Importance of Guiding the Work of Collaborative Teams

We have come to a deeper understanding of steps that schools can take to help teachers move from a tradition of isolation to a culture of collaboration; however, it has also become increasingly evident that simply providing educators with time to collaborate will do nothing to improve a school if they spend that time focusing on issues that do not impact student learning. One of the most pressing questions a school must consider as it attempts to build the collaborative culture of a PLC is not, "Do we collaborate?" but rather, "What do we collaborate about?"

8. The Importance of Widespread Leadership and the Role of the Central Office

Professional Learning Communities at Work focused on the school as the center of change and devoted little attention to the role of the central office in promoting the PLC concept throughout a district. Furthermore, although it called upon principals to involve faculty in decision making and to empower teachers and teams, it offered few specific examples regarding widespread distribution of leadership.

9. The Classroom as a Learning Community

In the past, we focused on restructuring schools to operate as PLCs. We have come to believe, however, that aspects of the concept can also be applied to the classroom. Restructuring classrooms to function as learning communities in their own right can provide the structure and climate for enhanced student learning, more effective teaching, and more positive relationships.

10. The Need for a Common Language

Harvard researchers Robert Kegan and Lisa Laskow Lahey (2001) found that changing the conversation in an organization can have a profound impact on its culture and the day-to-day work of the people within it. Changes in conversation, however, require specificity of language. Many organizations settle for superficiality in language, using terms so ambiguously and loosely that they can mean very different things to different people. We have come to understand that not only a common language but also precision regarding the meaning of that language are crucial to the culture of discipline essential to effective schools and districts.

11. The Benefit of a Contemporary Context

Much has changed in public education in the past decade. State standards have attempted to clarify what students must learn, state assessments are being used to monitor schools, and sanctions and penalties are now imposed upon schools and students on the basis of test results. No Child Left Behind legislation has been enacted and continues to be debated.

12. The Power of Stories

Richard Axelrod (2002) once wrote, "Universities come to know about things through studies, organizations come to know about things through reports, and people come to know about things through stories" (p. 112). Kouzes and Posner (1990) describe storytelling as "the most basic form of communication—more prevalent and powerful than facts and figures." They claim, "The strongest structure for any argument is a story" (p. 101). Howard Gardner (1990) argues that the artful creation and articulation of stories constitute a fundamental responsibility of leaders. Noel Tichy (1997) concurs that the ability to create and tell a vibrant story is one of the most powerful teaching tools available to leaders—"an essential prerequisite to becoming a first-class winning leader" (p. 174). In our own work with schools, we have found that stories are what people remember best, because good stories appeal to both reason and emotion—the head and the heart. Good stories teach us. They convey not only how something should be done but, more important, why it should be done. They communicate priorities and clarify what is significant, valued, and appreciated. Therefore we have integrated stories into many of the chapters of this book to help illustrate our points.

Søren Kierkegaard observed that while life must be lived forward, it can only be understood backward. Before moving forward with recommendations for transforming schools, we must examine the historical antecedents that have brought contemporary educators to this moment of opportunity.

REFERENCES

Axelrod, R. (2002). *Terms of engagement: Changing the way we change organizations.* San Francisco: Berrett-Koehler.

Carey, G., & Frohnen, B. (1998). (Eds.). *Community and tradition: Conservative perspectives on the American experience.* Lanham, MD: Rowman & Littlefield.

Clinton, W. (2007). Middlebury College graduation address, May 7, 2007. Retrieved February 18, 2009, from http://www.middlebury.edu/about/newsevents/archive/2007/newsevents_633158738134202567.htm

Collins, J. (2001). *Good to great: Why some companies make the leap . . . and others don't.* New York: Harper Business.

DuFour, R., DuFour, R., Eaker, R., & Many, T. (2006). *Learning by doing: A handbook for professional learning communities at work.* Bloomington, IN: Solution Tree.

DuFour, R., & Eaker, R. (1998). *Professional learning communities at work: Best practices for enhancing student achievement.* Bloomington, IN: Solution Tree (formerly National Educational Service).

Gardner, H. (1990). *Leading minds.* New York: Basic Books.

Kegan, R., & Lahey, L. (2001). *How the way we talk can change the way we work: Seven languages for transformation.* San Francisco: Jossey-Bass.

Kennedy, J. (1962, June 11). Commencement address at Yale University. Retrieved February 18, 2009, from http://www.jfklibrary.org/historical+resources/archives/reference+desk/speeches/jfk/003POF03Yale06111962.htm

Kouzes, J., & Posner, B. (1990). *Encouraging the heart.* San Francisco: Jossey-Bass.

Pfeffer, J., & Sutton, R. (2000). *The knowing-doing gap: How smart companies turn knowledge into action.* Boston: Harvard Business School.

Pfeffer, J., & Sutton, R. (2006). *Hard facts, dangerous half-truths and total nonsense: Profiting from evidence-based management.* Boston: Harvard Business School.

Saphier, J. (2005). *John Adams' promise.* Acton, MA: Research for Better Teaching.

Senge, P. (1990). *The fifth discipline: The art and practice of the learning organization.* New York: Currency Doubleday.

Senge, P., & Kofman, F. (1995). Communities of commitment: The heart of learning organizations. In S. Chawla & J. Renesch (Eds.), *Learning organizations: Developing cultures for tomorrow's workplace* (pp. 15–44). New York: Productivity Press.

Sergiovanni, T. (2005). *Strengthening the heartbeat: Leading and learning together in schools.* San Francisco: Jossey-Bass.

Tichy, N. (1997). *The leadership engine: How winning companies build leaders at every level.* New York: Harper Business.

Vonnegut, K. (1973). *Breakfast for champions.* New York: Delta Books.

CHAPTER NINE

Coaches as Leaders of Change

Jim Knight

I think that most teachers see their teaching as an art and when you're messing with their art, they can become really angry. And it's really hard not to take it personally. But I keep moving forward because I'm bringing better methods, and once I've given lots of backup, once they've started using it, once they see growth in their kids, they're OK.

—*Jean Clark, instructional coach,*
Bohemia Manor Middle School

The temptation is to avoid the leadership challenge altogether. Isn't it enough, we might ask, if instructional coaches (ICs) perform all the components of coaching (enroll, identify, explain, model, observe, explore, support, and reflect) in efficient and validating ways? Certainly a coach who does each of those tasks well is doing important and valuable work. The problem is that the complex challenges that require leadership refuse to leave coaches alone. ICs, sometimes on a daily basis, are thrown into situations where they will not be effective unless they lead. ICs need to shape team norms, facilitate schoolwide implementation of interventions, promote more constructive styles of professional discourse, motivate unmotivated teachers, raise thorny issues, negotiate resolutions to the conflicts that those thorny issues stir up, and stand in opposition to any action or attitude that is not good for children. Whether they like it or not, effective coaches must be effective leaders.

The concept of leadership carries with it many preconceptions. When we think of a leader, we often conjure up Hollywood images of men (usually) who exhibit heroic fortitude, courage, discipline, determination, and focus as they whip a bunch of losers into shape and overcome obstacles to fight the battle, take the flag, score the points, win at all costs, and beat the enemy. Clearly that notion of leadership is at odds with the partnership approach proposed for ICs.

When it comes to instructional coaching, a different concept of leadership is more appropriate. In line with recent studies of leadership, ICs need a paradoxical mix of humility and ambition (Collins, 2001), a desire to provide service that is at least as powerful as the drive to succeed (Greenleaf, 1998), a deep understanding of the emotional components of leadership (Goleman, Boyatzis, & McKee, 2002), and a recognition that a good leader must first be an effective teacher (Tichy & Cardwell, 2002). The reality is that instructional coaching usually demands leadership. The good news is that there are tactics (strategies or methods) that coaches can learn and employ that will increase their ability to lead change. This chapter focuses on eight high-leverage leadership tactics that coaches can employ to lead change in schools.

TACTIC 1: STAY DETACHED

Before she became an IC at Bohemia Manor Middle School in Cecil County, Jean Clark, one of the first winners of the Cecil County Teacher of the Year Award, was respected as a highly successful teacher. In fact, she was brought to Bohemia Manor by her principal, Joe Buckley, because he had personally experienced how effective she was. Nevertheless, despite her personal warmth and professional pedigree, Jean's first year at her new school was not all smooth sailing.

Jean came to Bohemia Manor excited about introducing Content Enhancement Routines and other research-based teaching practices to her teachers. An energetic and driven professional, she found it difficult to hide her enthusiasm for the teaching practices, and she fully expected her colleagues to see the value of focused planning and explicit teaching. Unfortunately, some teachers were not so quick to catch Jean's enthusiasm. In fact, not long after she started talking with staff, Jean observed that teachers were starting to avoid her in the halls, disparage her in the staff lounge, and going to great lengths to get out of her way. This wasn't easy for Jean to accept.

Talking about her experiences, Jean observed that "The decision to step forward and become a leader can be difficult because both professionally and personally you're moving away from your colleagues, and that's a very difficult thing—there's a lot of self-doubt and fear" (personal research, 2006).

Jean Clark

Jean Clark is an IC at Bohemia Manor Middle School in Cecil County, Maryland. She became an IC in 2004, but she says that she feels she has been a change agent for most of her professional life. Jean taught English for many years and was one of the first Cecil County Teachers of the Year. Jean is a certified Strategic Instruction Model Content Enhancement Professional Developer, a writer, and a poet.

Unfortunately, the resistance and personal attacks that Jean experienced are not uncommon. Ronald Heifetz and Marty Linsky (2002), in their book *Leadership on the Line: Staying Alive Through the Dangers of Leading,* observe that

> adaptive [complex] change stimulates resistance because it challenges people's habits, beliefs, and values. It asks them to take a loss, experience uncertainty, and even express disloyalty to people and cultures. Because adaptive change forces people to question and perhaps redefine aspects of their identity, it also challenges their sense of competence. Loss, disloyalty, and feeling incompetent: That's a lot to ask. No wonder people resist. (p. 30)

When people are nervous about change, they can feel compelled to resist and can give voice to that resistance by attacking the person promoting the change. By standing for a new vision of what a school or individual can be, by standing for change, ICs can inadvertently put themselves in the line of fire. And attack can be a very effective way to resist change. According to Heifetz and Linsky (2002),

"Whatever the form of attack, if the attackers can turn the subject of the conversation from the issue you are advancing to your character or style, or even the attack itself, it will have succeeded in submerging the issue" (p. 41).

Jean Clark found that teachers were inclined to attack her even after they had seen success. In her role as an IC, Jean reminded teachers of how they were falling short in their commitment to help children. Jean explains,

> Teachers might be using the Unit Organizer and the course map and starting to see kids that normally don't respond, responding. Even with that, they'll use it for a while and then stop using it because they need a lot of support or because they're very busy at home, and eventually they revert to the old way of take out your book and let me do round-robin reading. Then they become angry because I suspect they know that's not what they really want to be doing. And here comes Jean Clark and I'm going to throw a pallet at her. (personal research, 2006)

If coaches aren't attacked personally, they may find that their interventions come under attack. Even when programs are going well, when results are unmistakable, people in a school may find reasons to criticize a program. Unfortunately, what frequently occurs in schools is a vicious cycle that ensures that new teaching practices never get implemented—an "attempt, attack, abandon cycle" that prevents any real change from taking hold in schools. During the attempt, attack, abandon cycle, someone introduces a new practice into a school, and teachers make a half-hearted *attempt* to implement it. Then, before the program has been implemented effectively, and before it has been given sufficient time to be fully implemented, various individuals in the school or district begin to *attack* the program. As a result, many of the teachers implementing the program now begin to lose their will to stick with it. Inevitably, even though the practice was never implemented well, leaders in the district reject it as unsuccessful, and *abandon* it, only to propose another program that is sure to be pulled into the same vicious cycle, to eventually be attacked and abandoned for another program, and on and on. Thus, schools stay on an unmerry-go-round of attempt, attack, abandon, without ever seeing any meaningful, sustained change in instruction taking place (Knight, 2006).

| **Figure 9.1** | The Attempt, Attack, Abandon Cycle |

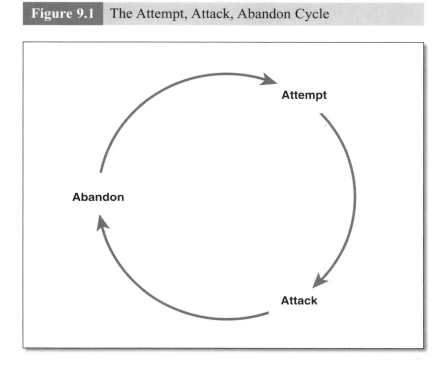

The Attempt, Attack, Abandon Cycle

What should coaches do when they come under attack? Jean Clark is unequivocal about how difficult it can be to encounter resistance: "I've been really depressed at times because I can't stand being the enemy." After interviewing Jean and other ICs across the nation and observing many coaches in action, I've come to believe that ICs have to "stay detached" to stay effective. If coaches become too personally involved in their change initiatives, if they see every attack on their program as an attack on themselves, they may find the personal consequences devastating. Jean says that she's "getting tougher" and learning to detach herself from each teacher's individual struggle to change and improve. "I'm getting tougher to where I can say, hey, let them go, this is the change stuff that you're seeing; you're seeing them blow up. It's a loss right now and they're grieving over a lot of stuff. Just get out of the way" (personal research, 2006).

I suggest four strategies ICs can employ to maintain a healthy distance when they are leading change.

1. *Use partnership communication.* This suggestion may seem paradoxical, or even contradictory. If partnership communication is all about building an emotional connection, how can ICs stay detached while also staying connected? In reality, it is paradoxical. The partnership approach grounds any act of communication in the belief that everyone's point of view should be listened to because everyone is equally valuable. Partnership communication helps us listen more effectively, empathize, and rethink communication from the perspective of the listener as opposed to our own point of view. ICs taking the partnership approach consciously build relationships by extending and turning toward others' emotional bids, and they are very aware of how their personal stories or the stories held by a listener can interfere with and sometimes stand in the way of any effective communication.

By taking the partnership approach, ICs can detach themselves by, first, proactively eliminating many of the time bombs that can blow up during interpersonal communication. Simply put, when teachers feel respected, when they are aware that their IC listens authentically, and when they feel an emotional connection with their IC, they are much less likely to attack the coach or the program. Paradoxically, therefore, the first step in staying detached is to reduce the number of attacks you might experience by taking the partnership approach.

2. *Change your thinking to create distance.* When Linda Stone, a former senior Microsoft executive, wrote out the most important lessons she'd learned in her life, she offered advice that seems highly pertinent to coaches trying to stay detached. Stone wrote,

> Whenever we feel defensive, hurt, personally attacked, confused, or afraid, we have a choice—we can get very curious. Rather than saying, "I never would have said that," we can say, "I wonder what these people heard me say? I wonder what their perception is?" (Jensen, 2005, p. 63)

Coaches can stay detached by reconceiving the attack as an opportunity to learn and better understand the people with whom they work.

3. *Keep it from being personal.* Perhaps the chief strategy ICs can use to stay detached is to be sensitive to the emotional undercurrents at work in any interchange. Then, if they notice an interaction turning negative, they can stay detached by recognizing what is happening and by telling themselves to keep their distance. William Ury (1985), more than two decades ago, referred to this tactic as "going to the balcony." He suggested that whenever we feel a conversation turning negative and personal, we can detach ourselves by imagining that we are watching the interaction from a balcony. Ury describes "going to the balcony" as follows:

> When you find yourself facing a difficult negotiation, you need to step back, collect your wits, and see the situation objectively. Imagine you are on a stage and then imagine yourself climbing onto a balcony overlooking the stage. The "balcony" is a metaphor for a mental attitude of detachment. From the balcony you can calmly evaluate the conflict almost as if you were a third party. . . . Going to the balcony means distancing yourself from your natural impulses and emotions. (1985, pp. 37–38)

The simple trick of imagining that we are physically distanced from the conversation can help us feel psychologically distanced from the interchange and help us avoid responding in ways we will later regret. One IC stays detached when things get heated simply by thinking, "Wow, this looks like one of those conflict situations; I wonder if I can use my communication techniques to keep this from escalating." The simple act of naming the situation as one with potential for conflict somehow provides the distance necessary for this coach to stay detached.

Coaches also need to ensure that their program or activities are not seen as their personal pet project. An additional part of "keeping it from being personal," then, is to ensure that we keep the focus on instruction and students and not on us. Although we want to build an emotional connection and want our colleagues to enjoy working with us, we do not want them to work with us out of personal obligation. If teachers try our practices merely because they feel they owe it to us, rather than because they believe it is good for kids or for them, eventually they will grow tired of spending their energy pleasing us. Coaches must resist the temptation to use their friendship as a leverage point for motivating colleagues and continually turn the focus of conversations to how strategies or teaching practices can help students.

4. *Take the long view.* Staying detached is not synonymous with being apathetic about results. In truth, it is just the opposite. If ICs are too personally involved in their project, they may find the unsuccessful days emotionally devastating. Furthermore, if the teaching practices proposed are tied too closely to the IC, that perception can further inhibit the spread of ideas in schools.

We believe that by staying detached, ICs increase the likelihood that interventions will catch on in a school. To effectively lead change, ICs sometimes need to consciously stand back from the potentially distressing moments of resistance that might keep them up late into the night. A better strategy is to take the long view, recognizing that research is quite clear that a well-organized coaching program should lead to widespread implementation and improvements in student achievements. By staying detached, by seeing beyond the momentary lapse and keeping the long-term goals in view, ICs can be more effective leaders of change.

TACTIC 2: WALK ON SOLID GROUND

ICs who are uncertain of their principles, goals, priorities, or practices may be unprepared for the turbulence and waves of resistance they may encounter in a school. ICs must be clear on what they stand for if they want others to stand with them in improving instruction for students. Henry Cloud (2006), in his book *Integrity: The Courage to Meet the Demands of Reality,* writes about the importance of being clear on who we are and what we stand for.

> People who do best in life have a well-defined identity on a number of fronts. They are secure in their boundaries, they know what they like and don't like, what they believe in and value, and they love and hate the right things. They are not wishy-washy and what psychologists call identity diffused, wondering who they are or what they are about, or thinking that they are everything. You get a good definition of who they are just from being around them. (p. 144)

A starting point for walking on solid ground is for ICs to work out their beliefs about the partnership principles of equality, choice, voice, dialogue, reflection, praxis, and reciprocity. ICs need to deeply understand these principles, first, so that they can decide whether or not they will ground their actions in them. If they do not agree with some of the principles, ICs should reflect and determine the principles that they will use as a foundation for action. Inevitably, ICs will be called upon to act in ways that are inconsistent with these principles (leading a change initiative that doesn't allow any room for teachers' choices, for example), and if they are unsure of their principles, they will have a harder time resisting such suggestions. They may also act in ways that will end up unsuccessful.

Jean Clark experienced the importance of walking on solid ground firsthand. When the program Jean was leading at Bohemia Manor Middle School began to gain momentum, administrators and teachers around the district started to ask her for the quick-fix version of Content Enhancement. She was invited to give a one-hour presentation to large groups of teachers, and to send materials to teachers without providing any kind of follow-up professional development. Jean's clarity about what she stood for, and her commitment to praxis and dialogue, helped her to say no. Because she knew what she stood for as a leader of professional learning, Jean was able to advocate for more effective forms of professional learning and keep the attempt, attack, abandon cycle from occurring, at least for the moment.

To stay grounded, coaches also need to stay fully conscious of the moral purpose that is at the heart of the work they do. As Michael Fullan (2003) observed,

> Moral purpose, defined as making a difference in the lives of students, is a critical motivator for addressing the sustained task of complex reform. Passion and higher order purpose are required because the effort needed is gargantuan and must be morally worth doing. (p. 18)

One way for coaches to walk on solid ground is to remind themselves—perhaps every day, hour, or minute—that the primary purpose of their work is to make life better for children.

To stand on solid ground, coaches also need to understand fully their long-term and short-term goals. Lynn Barnes, a coach at Jardine Middle School, sets goals for every week, making plans, for example, to speak briefly to three nonimplementers every five days. A useful practice for ICs before any meeting with a teacher or administrator is to ask, "What are my short-term goals for this interaction?" An IC's short-term goal with a teacher might be as simple as trying to enhance a relationship or as ambitious as getting someone on board to help lead a schoolwide reading program. When meeting with an administrator, a coach might set the short-term goal of always explaining a research-based teaching practice or explaining what someone should watch for while observing a teacher implement a new teaching practice.

As important as short-term goals are, an IC's long-term goals are even more important. Long-term goals provide focus and help ICs set priorities. Coaches who take the time to set long-term goals, and who monitor their progress, are better prepared to use their time efficiently. Simply put, coaches will lead change more effectively if they know their top priorities and have a clear understanding of the outcomes they hope to achieve. To lead teachers and schools in a given direction, coaches need to be clear on their destination.

Let me add a final word: Being sure of what you stand for is an essential part of being a leader, but steadiness is not the same thing as stubbornness. In our studies of ICs, we have found that having too firm a ground to stand on can be problematic if coaches become impervious to new ideas. Michael Fullan (2001) offers some excellent advice: "Beware of leaders who are always sure of themselves" (p. 123). Coaches need to remain open to new ideas, to learning from the teachers and administrators with whom they collaborate, or their lack of flexibility may keep others from working with them. Indeed, when coaches have reflected on and clarified what it is that they stand for, they may actually find it much easier to open their minds to other ways of understanding.

TACTIC 3: CLARIFYING YOUR MESSAGE

In addition to being clear about short- and long-term goals, ICs also need to be clear about the information and vision they want to share with teachers. Tichy and Cardwell (2002), whom *BusinessWeek* has rated as one of the "Top-Ten Management Gurus," considers such clarity to be an essential attribute of effective leaders. "Leaders," Tichy and Cardwell observe,

> must be able to share their experience. And in order to do that, they must externalize the tacit knowledge within them. They

must draw lessons from their experiences, and then convey those lessons in a form so that others can use it. (pp. 74–75)

Leaders intent on creating such learning conversations require what Tichy and Cardwell refer to as a *Teachable Point of View* (TPOV). A TPOV is a "cohesive set of ideas and concepts that a person is able to articulate clearly to others" (p. 74). Roger Enrico, from PepsiCo, has said that "A Teachable Point of View is worth 50 IQ points" (Tichy & Cardwell, 2002, p. 97).

Tichy and Cardwell describe four basic building blocks of a TPOV. First, a TPOV is built on central ideas. Ideas "enable the leader to create dynamic and engaging stories that detail where the company is, where it is going, and how they will get there" (p. 75). Second, a TPOV must include values that leaders can articulate explicitly to shape support for ideas. Third, a TPOV must be energizing, including "a clear set of beliefs and actions for motivating others" (p. 76). Finally, a TPOV involves what Tichy and Cardwell describe as "edge," "facing reality . . . and making tough decisions" (p. 76).

When Jean Clark began as an IC, she spent a great deal of time developing her own TPOV—though she likely wouldn't have used that terminology. Jean was determined to find effective ways to explain Content Enhancement—and that took time. "In the beginning," Jean said, "this stuff didn't make any sense." So, to make sense of Content Enhancement, Jean spent many hours reading through instructor's manuals, paraphrasing materials in her own mind, drawing semantic maps, and taking notes until she felt she knew the material. Jean also practiced teaching routines in the classroom so that she was fully aware of how it felt to teach students how to master concepts using the Concept Mastery Routine (Bulgren, Deshler, & Schumaker, 1993) or how to organize their units using the Unit Organizer Routine (Lenz, Bulgren, Schumaker, Deshler, & Boudah, 1994).

Jean found that "the smartest thing" was to take time to learn "a piece at a time." According to Jean, "You can't take this really quickly, you have to think about it." However, Jean's determination to get clarity about Content Enhancement is paying off: "I'm definitely changing as a result of this, and I'm really starting to get the big picture with Content Enhancement and the whole model, the whole Strategic Instruction Model." As she gets clearer, Jean finds she has become more capable of getting other teachers to implement the model. Jean reports, "Other people are having 'aha's'! All you need is one person to have an 'aha' every now and then; that's enough."

TACTIC 4: MANAGING CHANGE EFFECTIVELY

Buckingham and Coffman (1999), who studied more than 80,000 managers from different industries, suggest that a large part of effective leadership is effective management. These researchers sifted through literally millions of data sets, sorting and resorting until they synthesized the essence of effective management into six critical questions. These questions help us understand how ICs can perform many management tasks of leading change.

The Big Six

1. Do I know what is expected of me?
2. Do I have the materials and equipment I need to do my work right?
3. At work, do I have the opportunity to do what I do best every day?
4. In the past seven days, have I received recognition or praise for doing good work?
5. Is there someone at work who cares about me?
6. Is there someone at work who encourages my development?

Let's take a look at each of these questions as they apply to instructional coaching.

Do I Know What Is Expected of Me?

Teachers who do not understand what they have to do to implement a teaching practice may be quick to drop that practice when they find out it is not what they expected. Consequently, if ICs are unclear about what teachers need to do in order to implement practices, they run the risk of severely damaging a relationship they may have spent months or years developing. For example, a teacher trying out a new approach she learned from a coach who is blindsided by a time-consuming demand to grade learning sheets may quickly reject the approach or, perhaps even worse, reject the coach when she realizes the additional grading is more than she can handle.

To be effective, ICs have to be careful to explain exactly what teachers can expect while they try something new. Among other concerns, ICs should explain (a) what additional demands, if any, will be made on teacher time; (b) how much class time a given teaching practice will take; (c) how students might be expected to respond; (d) how the intervention fits with the district or state curriculum; and (e) what else may have to change for the practice to be implemented.

Do I Have the Materials and Equipment I Need to Do My Work Right?

Teachers tell us that one of the main reasons why they often do not implement new teaching practices is that they do not have the time or desire to put together all the materials necessary to try something new. ICs in Topeka and Baltimore have gotten around this barrier to implementation by giving teachers a cardboard box called "strategy in a box," filled with every item a teacher might need to implement a strategy or routine, including printed overheads, handouts or learning sheets for students, reading materials, or whatever else might be necessary for implementation. As IC Irma Brasseur has commented, "Part of our goal is to release teachers from burdensome, mundane things so they can spend time thinking about being a learner, to make changes to bring out critical teaching behaviors" (personal research, 2006).

At Work, Do I Have the Opportunity to Do What I Do Best Every Day?

Although coaches usually have little or no say in who teaches what classes, an IC can collaborate with teachers to make it possible for them to do their best every day. Most important, when coaches and individual teachers work together to identify instructional practices, they must be careful to identify interventions that build on the teacher's unique strengths. Teaching practices are not generic; what works well for one teacher might not work as well for another. The art of coaching is working together with a teacher to identify interventions that respond to the teacher's most pressing need while also taking advantage of the teacher's greatest strength.

In the Past Seven Days, Have I Received Recognition or Praise for Doing Good Work?

Recognizing and praising each teacher each week may be a stretch goal for some ICs, but that doesn't mean that it isn't a worthy one. As we've explained throughout this book, a coach is often much more effective if she can build an emotional connection with fellow teachers, and this includes recognizing, praising, and supporting teachers whenever possible. For Jean Clark, recognizing teachers also provides an opportunity for follow-up and dialogue: "If you don't have the follow-up and you don't have the opportunity to continually reuse it and talk about it and dialogue about it, it's not going to stick" (personal research, 2006).

Is There Someone at Work Who Cares About Me?

Can a coach be successful if he doesn't care about fellow teachers? I don't think so. Coaches who are truly collaborative can't help but find themselves in caring relationships with collaborating teachers. Interviews I've conducted with coaches across the nation have shown again and again that an important aspect of coaching is simply being available as a listener or a friend to fellow teachers. As IC Devona Dunekack has observed, being a coach is

> more than PD [professional development]. Every week, several times, people come and see me, shut the door and let go. They might talk about something personal or something in the school. I'm just a good listening ear, and after we've talked, they can get up and do the job that is extremely important to do. (personal research, 2006)

Is There Someone at Work Who Encourages My Development?

Ultimately, this is what an IC's primary work is, to continually encourage each teacher to develop, to be a better professional, to reach and encourage and support more children. As such, an effective IC contributes in immeasurable ways to the continual progress of the school. By facilitating the professional growth of their colleagues, coaches help teachers stay alive, stay growing, and stay effective shapers of children's lives.

Buckingham and Coffman's questions bring into focus some of the tactics, strategies, and perspectives an IC should employ, and the questions also demonstrate that having an IC in a school can be a powerful way to accelerate professional learning and, indeed, enable people to realize their potential and live meaningful lives. But managing is only part of leadership. To really lead change, you need to go further.

TACTIC 5: CONFRONTING REALITY

The most obvious leadership challenge may also be the most difficult: confronting reality. According to Bossidy and Charan (2004), who literally wrote the book on this topic, *Confronting Reality: Doing What Matters to Get Things Right,* "to confront reality is to recognize the world as it is, not as you wish it to be, and have the courage to do what must be done, not what you'd like to do" (pp. 6–7). But, recognizing and acting on the world as it is, is not always easy for ICs. When working one-to-one with teachers, for example, coaches may find it difficult to candidly discuss instructional practices because the way people teach is so intertwined with the way they define themselves. As a result, if I present an unattractive picture of the way a teacher delivers a particular lesson, for example, I may be criticizing an act that is at the heart of who that person is. To talk about teaching practice is to talk about one of the most personal parts of a teacher's life.

Recently, flying home from a work visit in Michigan, I had an experience that brought home to me just how difficult it can be to confront reality with others. When I sat down on the plane, I found myself sitting beside a fascinating man from the east coast. We quickly found ourselves talking about his work and his life, and I was impressed by the man's intellect, sense of humor, and wisdom. There was just one problem. His breath was terrible. Even though I really wanted to listen to this interesting man, I just couldn't get past the fact that his breath was so bad.

Always the coach, I began to be concerned about the many problems his breath might be causing. "I wonder," I thought, "if I should tell him about his problem. If this breath is a common problem. I wonder if this fellow is losing customers just because they can't stand the aroma emanating from his smiling face? I wonder what impact it has on his marriage and family? What does his wife think about this? I really should tell him about this problem so he can do something about it!" But I didn't say anything. The risks of upsetting this nice man, or getting him angry with me, seemed too great, and I just sat there listening—more concerned with getting along with him or avoiding conflict than I was with giving him some information that might have been very important.

My challenge on the plane is the challenge coaches face every day. ICs struggle to share information that is unpleasant at the same time that they work to maintain a healthy relationship with collaborating teachers. What is difficult one-to-one, where we are able to build strong, supportive bonds with individuals, is even more difficult at the group level. When we surface difficult truths in larger organizations like schools, not only do we have to address the personal issues that are an unavoidable part of confronting reality, we also have to deal with the other contingencies of life in organizations, such as incomplete data sources, misinformation arising from failure of internal communication, individuals who hide from their own professional failures, and so on. It's no wonder that Bossidy and Charan (2004) conclude that "Avoiding reality is a basic and ubiquitous human tendency" (p. 26).

Despite the seductive appeal of avoiding the truth, the fact is that schools won't move forward, and students' lives won't improve, unless ICs and other educational leaders ask some core questions about the teaching and learning that occurs in every classroom:

- What is it like to be a student in this classroom or school?
- How do the students feel in this class?
- Is this teacher using "hi-fi" teaching practices?
- Does the teacher appreciate, enjoy, and respect students?
- Are students engaged in this class?
- Are students having meaningful learning experiences, or are they simply completing tasks that fill the time?
- Does this class increase or decrease students' love of learning?
- Will students remember this class?

Along with questions about individual classes, coaches and educational leaders can confront reality by asking questions about the school and school culture:

- Are our teachers focused on becoming better teachers, or are they focused on making excuses?
- Is our school improving or declining?
- Do our teachers focus on students and teaching during team meetings, or do they focus on blaming, excuse making, or finger pointing?
- Are our leaders supportive and positive?
- Do our leaders encourage our teachers to meet high standards?
- Do our leaders walk the talk?

Confronting reality in most schools is tough, but failure to confront reality is much worse because it ensures that no meaningful improvement takes place. ICs can help a teacher or school face facts by asking some or all of these truth-seeking questions.

TACTIC 6: UNDERSTANDING SCHOOL CULTURE

More than two decades ago, researcher Susan Rosenholtz (1989) made the rather startling (to me at least) claim that "reality is socially constructed and maintained through everyday organizational life" and that "teachers shape their beliefs and actions largely in conformance with the structures, policies, and traditions of the workaday world around them" (pp. 2–3).

Rosenholtz identified shared goals, teacher collaboration, teacher certainty, learning enrichment opportunities, and teacher commitment as important attributes of effective schools. She adapted organizational theorist Rosabeth Moss Kanter's description of *stuck* and *moving* institutions to distinguish between effective and ineffective academic social organizations:

> The stuck feel no sense of progress, growth, or development and so tend to lower their aspirations and appear less motivated to achieve. They shy away from risks in the workplace and proceed in cautious, conservative ways. The moving, by contrast, tend to

recognize and use more of their skills and aim still higher. Their sense of progress and future gain encourages them to look forward, to take risks, and to grow. (Rosenholtz, 1989, p. 149)

The implications of Rosenholtz's research are provocative, suggesting that a teacher's effective or ineffective teaching practices result as much from where the teacher teaches as much as they do from who the teacher is. Thus, if you moved teachers from a stuck school to a moving school, just by virtue of where they worked, Rosenholtz suggests, they would in many cases become better teachers. When I share this research with educators, 25 years after Rosenholtz conducted it, these ideas still ring true.

Whether they fully agree with Rosenholtz or not, ICs need to attend to Rosenholtz's lesson: School culture can accelerate or inhibit change in numerous ways in schools. In a sense, culture functions like gravity, no one can see it, but it keeps things in place. In workshops, I often talk about the culture of the elevator. Somehow, most people in North America have mysteriously learned that that there are certain rules to being in an elevator. You know the rules: (a) don't talk, (b) face the door with your back to the wall, (c) look at the numbers. When I was an undergraduate student at the University of Ottawa in Canada, a young poet purposefully broke these rules, by standing with his back to the door, facing the other passengers in the elevator. Usually some people riding along became genuinely uncomfortable just by the way he stood in the elevator. It was as if these people were thinking, "Doesn't he know what the rules are?"

Such is the hold that culture can have over us. We come to act in regulated ways without really being aware that there are any regulations. When cultural norms are good for students, such as norms that say we never talk disrespectfully about children, we believe that all children can succeed, and we support professional learning, cultural norms can be positive. However, when cultural norms are not good for students, such as norms that say we blame the children and their parents for our unsuccessful students, we bully children, and we ridicule professional learning, then they can be very destructive.

One important leadership tactic, then, is for ICs to be sensitive to the cultural norms in a school and to work to change norms that are not good for students. By doing that, coaches function similarly to a group of leaders Debra Meyerson (2001) refers to as *tempered radicals.*

> Tempered radicals are people who operate on a fault line. They are organizational insiders who contribute and succeed in their jobs. At the same time, they are treated as outsiders because they represent ideals or agendas that are somehow at odds with the dominant culture. (p. 5)

One of the most important ways in which ICs can lead is by shaping the kinds of conversations that take place in schools. A coach intent on changing school culture must be what Kegan and Lahey (2002) refer to as *a discourse-shaping language leader* (p. 20). That is, he or she must stand for a new kind of conversation while at the same time staying a part of the school culture. Deborah Kolb and Judith Williams (2000) suggest that we redirect conversation away from unhealthy topics, like gossip, by using communication maneuvers they call *responsive turns.* Responsive turns are communication tactics ICs can use to redirect potential unhealthy conversations. I've included four responsive turns suggested by Kolb and Williams, along with my definitions and some examples.

TACTIC 7: BEING AMBITIOUS AND HUMBLE

When the teachers at Jean Clark's middle school resisted her suggestions and criticized her methods, Jean was tempted to return to the classroom and a simpler life. "I've always got one foot out the door," Jean said (personal research, 2006). But Jean did not give in to the seductive promise of a less stressful life. Rather, she stayed the course with the partnership approach. Jean employed a wide variety of relationship-building and communication strategies. She took time to meet one-to-one with teachers, talked with her colleagues about their day-to-day lives inside and outside of school, and listened authentically and with empathy.

At the same time, Jean refused to drift into the background. She was determined and driven—she sought out opportunities to bring together collaborating teachers to do coplanning with her, focusing on teachers who had informal power in her school. Jean also worked

Table 9.1   Responsive Turns

Tactic	What It Is	Example
Interrupt	Cutting off the negative conversation before it begins	"Oh crap, I'm late; I've gotta go."
Name	Describing what's going on so everyone can see it	"I just feel that if we keep complaining about kids, we're never going to come up with anything useful."
Correct	Clarifying a statement that is not true	"I was at the meeting, and Mr. Smith was actually opposed to the plan."
Divert	Moving the conversation in a different direction	"Speaking of Tom, when does the basketball season start this year?"

with her principal to set up afterschool professional development sessions and to encourage him to apply pressure on some teachers whom she thought might particularly benefit from instructional support. And she was also a voracious learner—attending courses, reading articles and books, and learning as much as she could, as quickly as possible, so that she had valuable, up-to-date knowledge to share with teachers. In short, Jean took a partnership approach with her teachers, but at the same time, she was willful, deliberate, and driven as she led change at her school.

Jean's combination of leadership and partnership slowly began to pay off, and she started to see improvements in the way teachers taught and students learned in her school and in her district as a result of her efforts. Indeed, in a matter of months, Bohemia Manor Middle School began to attract the attention of educators throughout Cecil County, and the impact of Jean's willful and respectful approach began to extend across the county.

Jean's approach is one that I have seen employed consistently by effective coaches in schools across America. To really make change happen, ICs employ the respectful, patient, and dialogical methods of the partnership approach. At the same time, they are driven, almost obsessive, about making significant changes happen. In his book *Good to Great,* Jim Collins (2001) has identified the same kind of paradoxical attributes in leaders of great organizations. When he looked for common traits among great companies, Collins explains, he was taken aback by what he found:

> We were surprised, shocked really, to discover the type of leadership required for turning a good company into a great one. Compared to high-profile leaders with big personalities who make headlines and become celebrities, the good-to-great leaders seem to have come from Mars. Self-effacing, quiet, reserved, even shy—these leaders are a paradoxical blend of personal humility and professional will. They are more like Lincoln and Socrates than Patton or Caesar. (p. 13)

Effective leaders, Collins (2005) reports, "are ambitious first and foremost for the cause, the movement, the mission, the work—not themselves—and they have the will to do whatever it takes . . . to make good on that ambition" (p. 11). Much the same can be said about effective ICs—they are very ambitious, but their ambition is for improvements in instruction and in the experiences of children in schools. "Success," Jean reports, "brings success . . . and it's starting to stick. There's a bunch of us doing it; we're becoming partners" (personal research, 2006).

TACTIC 8: TAKING CARE OF YOURSELF

Being a leader is emotionally challenging, and thousands of change agents have found it difficult to remain optimistic, energetic, and enthusiastic. When we are marginalized, attacked, or silenced, when our successes are downplayed and our contributions are overlooked, it is difficult to remain optimistic. As Heifetz and Linsky (2002) explain:

> When you lead people, you often begin with a desire to contribute to an organization or community, to help people resolve important issues, to improve the quality of their lives. Your heart is not entirely innocent, but you begin with hope and concern for people. Along the way, however, it becomes difficult to sustain those feelings when many people reject your aspirations as

too unrealistic, challenging, or disruptive. Results arrive slowly. You become hardened to the discouraging reality. Your heart closes up. (p. 226)

Too frequently, as the table below suggests, professionals in schools find it too difficult to maintain their own innocence, curiosity, and compassion. For ICs to remain emotionally healthy, given the challenges that can confront them in a school, they must take time to keep themselves healthy.

Table 9.2 Hope and Hopelessness When Leading Change

Quality of Heart	Becomes	Dressed up as
Innocence	Cynicism	Realism
Curiosity	Arrogance	Authoritative knowledge
Compassion	Callousness	The thick skin of experience

SOURCE: Heifetz & Linsky, 2002, p. 226

Distinguish Your Role From Your Self

Frequently, the kind of people who choose to become ICs are precisely those who are deeply invested in their role. Thus, coaches may tie their own sense of worth directly to their success or failure with teachers in school. When a teacher chooses to use a new practice that helps students be successful, these ICs may have a momentary blissful sense that they are competent, making a difference, and living a life that counts. Then, when teachers stop implementing change, resist change, or attack interventions, or even worse, ICs may feel a deep despair, questioning whether or not their work, or even their life, matters. Such profound emotional upswings and downturns can take a real toll on a coach's well being.

Heifetz and Linsky (2002) explain that leaders need to be careful to separate their "role" from their selves: "when you lead, people don't love you or hate you. Mostly they don't even know you. They love or hate the position you represent" (p. 198). To remain healthy, coaches need to remember this.

Find Confidants

Finding someone or a group of people to confide in is a positive way ICs can protect themselves and remain healthy. ICs, by virtue of their role, are often on their own in a school. They are often unable to immerse themselves completely in a school simply because they are always trying to change it. Coaches are in the school, but not of the school. As a result, they sometimes find themselves on the outside of the in-group, when the in-group is intent on gossiping, complaining, or blaming. For that reason, finding someone to confide in outside the school can be very helpful.

When Jean Clark was considering going back to her first love— the classroom—what kept her committed to being an IC was the development of a collaborative friendship with Sherry Eichinger, a special education teacher at Bohemia Manor Middle School. As the vignette below illustrates, Jean became an emotional and intellectual partner with Sherry. As is the case with true partnerships, Jean, the coach, gained from collaborating with Sherry as much or more as Sherry, the teacher, gained from Jean.

Faith

In the years previous, I was training to be a professional developer. But I had this fear that maybe I don't have good people skills, perhaps I shouldn't be doing this. I kept running into these adults who were getting really ticked off at me. I kept thinking, "Well, you know, I'm just getting more and more awkward here as I'm aging and I'm not able to get these folks to work with me as I used to." So I was just about ready to get out of this field and go back to the classroom.

But what I've been discovering is that I can do this really, really well as long as I have partners. I see that when I have a partner like Sherry. She was a Christi McCollum scholar. She has a master's in special ed and in transitions, and she will not back off for those kids—she will do lots of work. I gained a great deal to suddenly be around someone who works like that. She started coming to me and asking, "Well, how would you teach a kid that really didn't understand how to read?" and "I don't understand how to do this," and every time she asked me a question, I had to think about it, and as soon as I started to think about it, I started thinking about how I learned.

(Continued)

(Continued)

The two of us work so well together. We disagree with one another at times, but we're both working for the same thing; we're both working for the kids and an understanding with the kids. I can't do it by myself, and I see that she can't do it by herself. We support one another. She supports me emotionally when I'm really depressed; she tries to keep me up. And when she's really depressed, thinking, "OK, I'm not going to do this another year, everybody's at my throat," I talk to her about it and remind her how far we've come. So we support one another both cognitively and emotionally. Because it's hard to do this work without a partner.

Being a change agent, you can weather it, you can weather what happens to you if you have enough folks talking to you—not just talking to you, but giving you things to think about, and letting you see their growth, like I've seen her growth. Having her there, it has given me faith. (personal research, 2006).

Find Sanctuary

The need to build in a time and place to recharge your batteries is not a new idea. In as ancient a document as Genesis in the Bible, we were advised to ensure that we take one day off from all of our work. Researchers studying top athletes have found that that biblical advice still holds true for active athletes. Loehr and Schwartz (2003), for example, have conducted studies of the attributes of great athletes. When they compared great athletes with good athletes, they found that great athletes don't try any harder or, in many cases, aren't any more skilled than good athletes, but they are much better at building variety into their training routine.

I believe that ICs can take a page from the great athletes that Loehr and Schwartz describe. Coaches, like athletes, need to be sure to build in opportunities to relax, refresh, and recharge. Jean Clark reports that she's fully aware that she does need to take care of herself, and she has her ways to relax and renew herself that work best for her. "I'm a writer; I write constantly. I read all the time, I go to counseling. I'm in 12-step meetings, you name it . . . I go to church . . . I do everything to stay emotionally healthy" (personal research, 2006).

One simple way to recharge is to find a place where you are able to relax and cool your heels, so to speak. Your own personal sanctuary might be your favorite coffee shop downtown, a park bench, a quiet out-of-the-way corner in the library, or the swing on your front porch. What matters is that you find a place where you feel free to relax and let your mind stand at ease for an hour or two. I don't own a condo by the ocean or a cabin by a mountain stream, but I have found my own way to find sanctuary. In Lawrence, Kansas, where I live, there is a five-mile concrete trail that provides bikers, runners, and Rollerbladers with a quick route out of town and into a beautiful, wide prairie meadow. My sanctuary is to tie up my old pair of Rollerblades, program my iPod to play whatever music suits me on a given day, and roll out into the valley. For an hour or so with my Rollerblades, music, and the nature trail, I'm able to put the pressing deadlines and other challenges I face on hold and simply rest and relax. Indeed, many of the ideas that have found their way into this book first flew into my consciousness when I was far away from my computer, blading through the valley just outside of Lawrence.

THE FINAL WORD ON JEAN CLARK AND BOHEMIA MANOR MIDDLE SCHOOL

During the last weeks of Jean's first year at Bo Manor, I was sitting in my office at the University of Kansas. When my phone rang, I picked it up and heard the voice of Joe Buckley, Jean's principal, on the other end of the line. Joe had never called me; in fact, I had never given him my telephone number, but he told me that he had gone out of his way to get it from Jean. "Jim," he said, "we've just gotten our test scores, and let me read some of them to you." Joe quickly rattled off some scores that, I learned, showed that in each grade, the number of students who were proficient in math and reading had doubled. Bohemia Manor School, it turns out, was the only school in Cecil County in which a majority of students were proficient in all subjects at all grade levels. The results were, as Joe said, "amazing." "Jim," he concluded, "I just had to call you to thank you for your work supporting Jean. These scores just show how important she is to this school. She's done an awesome job this year."

Throughout that year, I had worked with Jean, and I knew what struggles she had gone through to win over her school and to make meaningful improvements in instruction to take root. When I heard how genuinely grateful and excited her principal was, I felt a deep sense of satisfaction. Jean had stuck it out, weathered the attacks, and led her school forward, and in the end, her school's students were clearly better for her work. Working as an IC, Jean had had an unmistakable, positive impact on the teachers in her school, and consequently, the students in her school were learning more and performing better. What could be better than that?

GOING DEEPER

Reading about leadership is a bit like reading about surfing, I imagine. Books might help, but you really have to dive in and get wet to truly benefit from your readings. Most readers of this book, I suspect, are already confronting leadership challenges. In that case, the following sources should prove helpful.

Michael Fullan's books are a great starting point for the study of leadership.

Heifetz and Linsky's (2002) *Leadership on the Line: Staying Alive Through the Dangers of Leadership* accurately summarizes many of the emotionally taxing challenges a leader might face and offers practical strategies people can use to overcome those challenges. Heifetz and Linsky also explain how and why leaders should distinguish between technical and adaptive challenges.

Goleman, Boyatzis, and McKee's (2002) *Primal Leadership: Learning to Lead With Emotional Intelligence* applies the concept of emotional intelligence, first introduced by Daniel Goleman, to leadership. The authors contend that a leader's most important task, the primal task, is to address the emotional needs of those being led. Leaders who are astute enough to guide their teams to experience positive emotions are referred to as *resonant leaders*. The model of leadership they propose is consistent with the partnership principles, and the book's description of the relationship-building skills, leadership styles, and strategies necessary to create resonant leadership are very useful. The book also contains some excellent nonexamples.

When I heard Dennis Sparks speak in 2005, he held up a copy of *Primal Leadership* and said, "If there is one book on leadership that educators should read, this is it." Some might make a claim that the same could be said for his book, *Leading for Results: Transforming Teaching, Learning, and Relationships in Schools* (2005). This is a remarkably concise work that contains 25 strategies people can employ to refine their leadership skills. Sparks's visionary *and* practical strategies include a variety of ways to clarify and achieve your goals, several suggestions for developing clear thinking, skills for improving authentic listening and encouraging dialogue, and other strategies leaders can employ to walk the talk as they lead.

Henry Cloud's (2006) *Integrity: The Courage to Meet the Demands of Reality* is a very readable but wise and useful book that describes six qualities that determine leadership success in business (I believe his suggestions also apply to the social sector). The six qualities are establishing trust, orienting toward truth, getting results, embracing the negative, orienting toward increase, and orienting toward transcendence.

Marcus Buckingham and Curt Coffman's (1999) *First, Break All the Rules: What the World's Greatest Managers Do Differently* introduces the Big Six Questions included in this chapter. Based on over 80,000 interviews conducted by the Gallup Organization, the book describes three basic strategies used by outstanding managers. First, in managing, leading, and "sustained individual success," the most productive leaders find the talents of people they work with and do not dwell on their negative aspects. Second, managers shape jobs to fit people, rather than shape people to fit jobs. Third, they are crystal clear in expectations and goals. Fourth, leaders choose employees for the talent they have, not just their expertise.

TO SUM UP

- Leadership is an unavoidable part of instructional coaching.
- There are eight tactics ICs can use to increase their effectiveness as leaders:

Stay detached: Find ways to take the long view and keep yourself from being overly invested in each component of your coaching program.

Walk on solid ground: Know what you stand for if you want others to stand with you.

Clarify your message: Develop a deep understanding and clear way of communicating the ideas you have to share with others.

Be ambitious and humble: Embody a paradoxical mix of ambition for students and personal humility.

Confront reality: Ask questions that help you focus on the real situation in teachers' classrooms and in your school.

Understand school culture: Recognize that behavior is often as much a product of organizational culture as it is of each individual's characteristics.

Manage change effectively: Do all you can to ensure that your teachers know what is expected of them and have what they need to implement the teaching practices you share with them.

Take care of yourself: If you want to lead change, you must protect and nourish yourself.

NOTE

1. At the end of Jean's second year, Bohemia Manor again showed more growth than any other middle school in Cecil County.

REFERENCES

Bossidy, L., & Charan, R. (2004). *Confronting reality: Doing what matters to get things right.* New York: Random.

Buckingham, M., & Coffman, C. (1999). *First, break all the rules: What the world's greatest managers do differently.* New York: Simon & Schuster.

Bulgren, J. A., Deshler, D. D., & Schumaker, J. B. (1993). *The concept mastery routine.* Lawrence, KS: Edge Enterprises.

Cloud, H. (2006). *Integrity: The courage to meet the demands of reality.* New York: HarperCollins.

Collins, J. (2001). *Good to great: Why some companies make the leap . . . and others don't.* New York: HarperCollins.

Collins, J. (2005). *Good to great and the social sector: A monograph to accompany good to great.* Boulder, CO: Collins.

Fullan, M. (2001). *Leading in a culture of change: Being effective in complex times.* San Francisco: Jossey-Bass.

Fullan, M. (2003). *Change forces with a vengeance.* New York: RoutledgeFalmer.

Goleman, D., Boyatzis, R., & McKee, A. (2002). *Primal leadership: Learning to lead with emotional intelligence.* Boston: Harvard Business School Press.

Greenleaf, R. K. (1998). *The power of servant-leadership.* San Francisco: Berrett-Koehler.

Heifetz, R. A., & Linsky, M. (2002). *Leadership on the line: Staying alive through the dangers of leading.* Boston: Harvard Business School Press.

Jensen, B. (2005). *What is your life's work? Answer the big questions about what really matters . . . and reawaken the passion for what you do.* New York: HarperCollins.

Kegan, R., & Lahey, L. (2002). *How the way we talk can change the way we work: Seven languages for transformation.* San Francisco: Jossey-Bass.

Knight, J. (2006). Instructional coaching: Eight factors for realizing better classroom teaching through support, feedback and intensive, individualized professional learning. *The School Administrator, 63*(4), 36–40.

Kolb, D. M., & Williams, J. (2000). *The shadow negotiator: How women can master the hidden agendas that determine bargaining success.* New York: Simon & Schuster.

Lenz, B. K., Bulgren, J., Schumaker, J., Deshler, D. D., & Boudah, D. (1994). *The unit organizer routine.* Lawrence, KS: Edge Enterprises.

Loehr, J. S., & Schwartz, T. (2003). *The power of full engagement: Managing energy, not time, is the key to high performance and personal renewal.* New York: Free Press.

Meyerson, D. E. (2001). *Tempered radicals: How people use difference to inspire change at work.* Boston: Harvard Business School Press.

Rosenholtz, S. J. (1989). *Teacher's workplace: The social organization of schools.* New York: Teachers College Press.

Sparks, D. (2005). *Leading for results: Transforming teaching, learning, and relationships in schools.* Thousand Oaks, CA: Corwin.

Tichy, N. M., & Cardwell, N. (2002). *The cycle of leadership: How great leaders teach their companies to win.* New York: HarperBusiness.

Ury, W. (1985). *Getting past no: Negotiating your way from confrontation to cooperation.* New York: Bantam.

CHAPTER TEN

Developing and Sustaining School Principals

Lessons From the Greater New Orleans School Leadership Center

Kenneth Leithwood

Scott Bauer

Brian Riedlinger

INTRODUCTION

Being a principal is tough work—rewarding for many, but tough for all. In some locations, attitudes toward school leadership seem paradoxical. Reformers, members of the public, and many education professionals, for example, view principals as absolutely key to successful school improvement, even when such improvement is initiated by others (e.g., Wikeley, Stoll, Murillo, & De Jong, 2005). At the same time, salaries paid to principals in many U.S. states, at least, offer almost no material incentive for teachers to seriously consider volunteering to work the additional 15 or 20 hours per week that has become the norm for today's principals (Harvard Education Letter, 2000). Not to mention being the person squarely in the sights of the accountability militia howling after what sophisticated analysts (e.g., Linn, 2003) argue are often impossible "adequate yearly progress" targets for student achievement on high-stakes tests in schools set by states and districts.

While many principals like what they do and report high levels of job satisfaction (e.g., Malone, Sharp, & Walter, 2001), working conditions notwithstanding, many also report feeling worn out by the job, isolated, and under considerable stress and seriously ponder the prospects of alternative employment (Whitaker, 2003). We can't afford to have them leave; many districts are already forced to appoint people with minimal experience, at best. Nor can we afford to have them stay while feeling burned out. Burnout manifests itself in resistance to change and innovation, insensitive social relationships, and lack of care for others. So, it is past time that we attended more deeply to the problem of sustaining and further developing the principals we now have in schools.

In this chapter, we describe the lessons learned about sustaining and further developing principals from the past six years work of the *Greater New Orleans School Leadership Center* (SLC). With the support of a local foundation (the Baptist Community Ministries), the SLC's work was the object of an extensive, six-year external evaluation. This evaluation produced a series of quarterly reports about participants', or "fellows'," experiences in Center activities, the influence of those experiences on their work in schools, and the effects of that work on student engagement and academic achievement. Evidence collected for that evaluation included direct observations of the Center's work, interviews with fellows about the value they attributed to that work, surveys conducted with teachers in fellows' schools, surveys of students about their engagement in fellows' schools, and analyses of changes in the achievement of students in fellows' schools using the results of state-administered achievement tests.

Over that six-year period, the SLC found multiple ways of connecting its work to the professional and personal needs of an ever-expanding group of principals in the region. The Center also found increasingly effective ways of ensuring that its work made a significant contribution to the quality of teaching and learning in fellows' schools. By any reasonable standard, the SLC must be judged a major success and one of the few organizations that can lay claim to having a sustained, long-term impact on a well-defined population of schools, teachers, administrators, and students.

There is much to be learned from the SLC's work about building and sustaining the motivations, commitments, and capacities of practicing school leaders. Our first initiative to ensure lessons from that work did not go unnoticed focused on the relationship between SLC initiatives and student academic achievement (Leithwood, Riedlinger, Bauer, & Jantzi, 2003). Our second initiative, described in this chapter, aimed to better understand the effects of the SLC's work on the type of leadership principals provided to their schools, as well as the energy and commitments they developed for carrying out that leadership. Evidence used for this purpose came from a series of 12 case studies of principals and schools. The 12 principals had participated in SLC initiatives for at least three years during which time their schools had demonstrated improvements in teaching and learning. School staffs attributed a significant portion of that improvement to the principals' leadership and principals attributed much of their impact on participation in SLC experiences.

State-collected student achievement data were the starting point for selecting the 12 schools. All schools demonstrating increases in state testing results over a three-year period were included in the initial pool of potential schools for the study. Data from the larger external evaluation provided additional information, including results of teacher and student surveys conducted on two occasions several years apart in each school. These surveys captured teachers' judgments about the leadership and management of the principal, as well as the condition of school characteristics key to school improvement efforts. Student data, in addition to academic achievement, were about their engagement in their school. Interviews were conducted with principals and teachers in each of 12 selected schools during the fall of 2004. All interviews were transcribed and coded according to questions included in the interview protocol.

SLC INITIATIVES FOR DEVELOPING AND SUSTAINING PRINCIPALS

The SLC program reflects several sources of advice about leadership development strategies. One of these sources is the National Staff Development Council (Sparks & Hirsh, 2000). The Council recommends that leadership development programs have the following features: They should be long-term rather than episodic, job-embedded rather than detached, carefully planned with a coherent curriculum, and focused on student achievement. Programs should also emphasize reflective practice, provide opportunities for peers to discuss and solve problems of practice, and provide a context for coaching and mentoring.

Based on data provided by the University Council on Educational Administration (UCEA), Peterson (2001) argues that programs must have a clear mission and purpose linking leadership to school improvement, a coherent curriculum that provides linkage to state certification schemes, and an emphasis on the use of information technologies. He also suggests that programs should be continuous or long-term rather than one-shot, and that a variety of instructional methods should be used rather than relying on one or a small set of delivery mechanisms.

SLC's program explicitly reflects these sources of advice about the features of successful leadership development experiences. It also is unique among North American leadership centers in several important respects. First, the mission and goals of the SLC squarely connect the work of the principal to improving student achievement. In sharp contrast to traditional principals' centers, which typically focus on leadership development as an end in itself and take as an act of faith that participants will use newfound skills to improve schools, the SLC has been committed to school improvement through leadership development from the outset. The SLC places a strong emphasis on giving principals and other school leaders the skills, resources, and tools that are needed to thoughtfully improve teaching and learning in their schools. This translates into a focus on changing how teachers teach and how they look at their teaching; an examination of supervision practices; and activities that focus on school change, school reform, and improving pedagogy. The Center deals with leadership skills and practices only insofar as a research-based theory of action can be articulated connecting these practices to school improvement. Significantly, the SLC's focus on leadership for school improvement is so deeply ingrained that it employs an evaluation design that looks at indicators of student performance and achievement as the ultimate litmus test of its efficacy.

The SLC is also unique because it has a full-time staff and operates as an independent, not-for-profit organization governed through a partnership of the funder Baptist Community Ministries (BCM), the

University of New Orleans, and Xavier University of Louisiana. Headed by the President/CEO, the Center staff also includes the Fellows Director, the Research Director and Research Associate, and a cadre of part-time graduate student interns. Support staff includes an Events Coordinator and Office Manager. The governance structure includes a board of directors made up of six representatives selected by the funder (BCM), and three representatives selected by each university. Each participant organization on the board has included experienced school principals among its board representatives. All significant decisions in the Center are made by a structure that includes fellows, including a team that selects each new cohort of SLC participants.

The staffing and governance structure are a product of two key principles stressed by the original Center design team. First, the team stressed the importance of the Center "being there" for principals. The norm experienced by most principals to be served by the Center was that support (when there was any at all) was sporadic and based on other peoples' notions of what principals need; there was a growing consensus that high-quality professional development needs to be continuous. In any case, the team's assumptions about the nature of school change suggested that if the goal was to improve schools, SLC initiatives could not be one-shot and disconnected from the experience of principals and their schools. The governance structure also aimed to ensure that Center activities were relevant by principals' standards. All programs have been designed with fellows, guided by the expressed needs of principals and their schools, and each member of the Center staff is in contact with fellows through shared decision-making teams. Indeed, the original design for Center programs was a product of a team of 13 "founding fellows," who worked with university faculty and the foundation to conduct research on existing leadership development center models and create the initial model for the SLC.

The Center's program reflects a mix of traditional and somewhat novel activities and services. Programs have been designed around shared beliefs about the impact of leadership on school improvement, promotion of social justice, and the transformation of schools into learning organizations. The Center attempts to model for fellows the kinds of activities and practices that principals are encouraged to incorporate into their schools. There are four primary program areas.

The Fellows' Program

The fellows' program is the heart of the Center's activities. Rather than involving principals sporadically in isolated activities, a cadre of approximately 24 principals a year—from area public, private, and parochial schools—apply to be fellows in the SLC. Fellowship reflects the primary way the Center strives to build a network among school leaders. Acceptance of a fellow's position carries significant rights and responsibilities.

Fellows are selected each January. Each fellow signs a contract committing to participate in certain activities that are designed to focus his/her attention on leadership development for school improvement. In their first year, fellows participate in three preinstitute staff development programs that deal with vision building, school improvement, and knowledge building through analysis of school performance data. Second, fellows participate in two weeklong summer institutes that build on the preinstitutes. These institutes focus on enriching leader's ideas about quality teaching and how leadership can promote it. Fellows are polled after the summer institute on their schools' needs so that postinstitute sessions can be designed and conducted to have maximum impact on school goals. Third, fellows are given a sizable grant ($10,000) to use to supplement the implementation of some facet of their schools' improvement plan. Center staff works with each fellow to ensure that these moneys are targeted for significant student impact and that plans have a sound evaluation component. Fourth, fellows each receive a laptop (more recently, a tablet) computer and training in accessing the Internet in an effort to encourage them to develop skills in the use of technology.

Originally, the fellowship was intended to last for two years. An indicator of the programs' impact, however, is that past fellows have essentially refused to leave. They created a membership category, "veteran fellow" (some of whom call themselves "fossil fellows"), structured an ongoing program (including their own summer institute), and serve as volunteers to help facilitate other SLC events.

Conferences and Workshops

The SLC sponsors three types of conferences and workshops, which are open to all administrators in the five-parish region. Each fall and spring, the center sponsors a one- or two-day institute on a topic deemed important by fellows. For example, in the fall of 2004, the Center sponsored a two-day session on teaching children of poverty. Over 200 educators attended. The SLC also sponsors more frequent "conversations," small gatherings of principals who have an opportunity to speak informally to an acknowledged expert (who is typically visiting New Orleans for another reason). Finally, the Center staff also makes itself available for districts, schools, and other professional organizations for customized workshops and act as a conduit for schools to access university scholars and national experts for workshops.

Research Services

In an effort to promote high-quality decision making and the active use of school performance data, the SLC maintains a full-time research office, possibly the only school leadership center in the nation to invest significant resources in this fashion.

The research office provides several services, by far the most used of which is the preparation of research briefs on request. A research brief is a short literature review on any question or problem identified by a fellow, including an executive summary of research, an annotated bibliography and copies of one or two relevant papers. The SLC has a full-time research associate and a staff of graduate assistants from partner universities to provide this service. To date, the Center has developed over 180 briefs, and a library of briefs is maintained so that fellows can request reprints (which are updated after one year). This service allows fellows to assess the extent of evidence available in support of the effects on student learning of initiatives they may be planning in their schools.

The research office also assists fellows in two other ways. First, small research grants are available to fellows' schools to conduct action research; about twenty grants were commissioned in the Centers' first three years. Second, Center staff is available to schools and local districts to conduct research projects, prepare summaries of school performance data, and otherwise connect the schools to the services of partner universities. The research office also oversees maintaining the Center's modest lending library of books, videotapes, and other audiovisual material.

Learning Initiatives

The newest facet of the SLC's program offerings is the Learning Initiatives (SLC-LI), started three years ago as a result of fellows' input and ideas generated with the external evaluator. In the Learning Initiatives, which new fellows must participate in as a part of their fellowship commitment, principals work together with their school leadership team on the design, implementation, and evaluation of their school's annual improvement plan. SLC-LI schools work in loose collaboration with other SLC schools that have targeted similar, student focused, school improvement objectives, and they receive facilitated training, data disaggregation services, and support for implementation and evaluation of school plans. Teachers' leaders learn more about powerful forms of instruction. This learning is then shared with colleagues in the school, and support for implementing such instruction is provided by schools leaders. Of all the components of the SLC program, this one addresses instructional improvement most directly.

Other Activities

More recently, the SLC has added to its repertoire leadership development programs for aspiring principals and teacher leaders, as well as a new program for superintendents and other central office administrators focused on the districts' role in supporting school change. The center is also working with school systems to develop a coaching and supervision program for new principals, which will replace the existing state-supported internship. These programs help leaders improve their schools by concentrating their leadership on teaching and learning.

LESSONS ABOUT HOW TO DEVELOP AND SUSTAIN PRINCIPAL LEADERSHIP

We identified ten lessons for developing and sustaining principal leadership from our 12 case schools. These lessons, we believe, should be of considerable interest to the vast network of policy makers, program developers, district leaders, foundations, universities, professional associations, and staff developers across the world who are convinced that the success of their school reform efforts hinges on improving and sustaining the quality of school leadership. These lessons should be viewed both as a source of optimism that such improvement is possible and a source of guidance about how to go about the task.

Lesson One: Dramatic Individual Change Is Possible

Extended and intensive professional development experiences for principals outside their own school and district environment can have a powerful influence on how principals approach improvement in their schools and their own leadership. Professional development of this sort seems capable of dramatically altering what are typically thought to be "entrenched" leadership styles, often described as "autocratic," in favor of much more democratic and participatory styles. Recent evidence in support of this lesson can be found in other, quite different, contexts (e.g., Menter, Hollingan, & Mthenjwa, 2005).

One of our case study principals, for example, had this to say about her approach to leadership and how it changed as a result of SLC experiences: "Before SLC, I don't want to say that I was a dictator, but I definitely made all or most of the decisions here at school" (personal correspondence, 2005). SLC, she believed, taught her the importance of delegating authority and sharing decision making (although ultimately she believed that it was still she who had to make the final decision). Because she began to understand that she could not do everything herself, she formed committees to handle many functions that were previously handled by her and the assistant principal; committees were formed to handle awards, discipline, grandparents' day, voluntary sponsorship, and social activities. This principal felt less stress because of shared leadership. She also believed that her faculty were more cohesive. Because they are more involved in decision making, "they are buying into what we are doing here at school. We're all in it together." The teachers we interviewed corroborated this view. "Before, we did things because we were told we had to do them; now we have more input and our input is heard and valued." The principal "has made us realize that we all have to pull together as a team to be successful" (personal correspondence, 2005).

Lesson Two: One Good Experience Can "Jump Start" the Adoption of a Continuous Learning Ethos

A small number of highly positive professional development experiences, most of our school cases suggest, can create a heightened interest in continuous learning on the part of principals and more self-initiated participation in subsequent professional development. Indeed a few highly positive experiences seem capable of reversing the negative attitudes toward professional development that may have resulted from unhelpful prior experiences, of which most teachers and administrators seem to have had many. For example, when one of our case study principals first began to attend SLC initiatives, she was getting tired of her school leadership role; things had become "difficult" for her. But "The School Leadership Center helped rekindle my spark" (personal correspondence, 2005). Indeed it reawakened her desire to go back to graduate school, something she didn't think she was going to do. From her perspective, the SLC encouraged principals to be "on the look out" for something that will keep them engaged when things get difficult. Following this advice, this principal found an issue that she felt the need to understand more fully—the impact on a child's life of having a mother who is in prison. She believed that the SLC was always there to encourage her to keep going—to develop a passion for something.

Lesson Three: Ongoing Support Is Needed If Leaders Are to Influence Student Learning

The change management literature is fond of telling us that change requires both pressure and support. But in the current context of accountability-oriented education policies, the balance between the two, experienced by many school leaders, including Center fellows, is radically one-sided. Professional development that helps principals cope effectively with the pressure may be the most defensible form of support for them.

The greatest efforts of high-quality, intensive, professional development for principals are realized when initial professional development experiences are extended and reinforced through well-planned follow-up support over several years. The school cases teach us the importance of ongoing relationships with the SLC staff, a network of other school leaders with similar challenges and, occasionally, "outsiders" who bring unique perspectives to bear on the principals' work. As one of our case study fellows noted, the opportunity to be with other school leaders and learn from them was most helpful to her. To see that her struggles were no different from those of other principals, regardless of type of school (private, parochial, or public, urban or suburban) was a real eye-opener for her. "We are all dealing with similar issues." She believed that the SLC stressed the importance of networking and the power of conversations to "help sustain, encourage, and support us. They help us celebrate when good things happen and lift us up when bad things happen" (personal correspondence, 2005). The SLC staff, through the SLC-LI in particular, not only provided skill-oriented training to principals and leadership teams, they also acted as a "critical friend,"

> a trusted person who asks provocative questions, provides data to be examined through another lens, and offers critiques of a person's work as a friend. A critical friend takes the time to fully understand the context of the work presented and the outcomes that the person or group is working toward. The friend is an advocate for the work. (Costa & Kallick, quoted in Swaffield, 2005, p. 44)

Lesson Four: Training Should Encompass the Team as Well as the Individual Principal

Follow-up experiences are most useful when they focus directly on issues in the principal's school and include direct training of school staff in addition to the principal, typically a cross-role leadership or improvement team. This more inclusive training is a way of sharing with the principal the job of developing leadership capacities among others in the school, as well as helping transform the school into a professional learning community. SLC's Learning Initiative adopted this inclusive focus, and most of our school cases celebrate the outcomes of that focus.

One of the case study principals explained that from the distance of a few years she realized that what was most helpful was participating in SLC-LI, "where we were given the time and space to work with our teachers on our School Improvement Plan" (personal correspondence, 2005). SLC-LI provided an opportunity, she noted, to share ideas and strategies with other teachers who had similar concerns. This sharing of ideas, the principal believed, helped to build teacher leaders who then took on more responsibilities at the school.

SLC-LI combined sessions that encouraged cross-school and cross-district problem solving with work in fellows' own schools, thereby encouraging a level of sharing typically not experienced by principals and teacher leaders. Three outcomes seem noteworthy from this: a greater appreciation for the normalcy of problems and dilemmas faced across schools, an increased openness to alternative ways of looking at these problems, and a high level of transparency with regard to the discussion of problems and their possible solutions.

This lesson acknowledges our growing understanding about the contribution that shared leadership makes to school improvement (e.g., Chrispeels, 2004), how shared leadership is best developed (Frost & Durrant, 2004), and, perhaps especially, how school improvement initiatives can be sustained during leadership transitions (Lambert, 2005).

Lesson Five: Direct, Practical Help in Data-Driven Decision Making Is Especially Critical in the Current Policy Environment

Principals are being widely admonished to be data-driven in their decision making (e.g., Earl & Katz, 2002) but are often constrained by lack of time, capacity, and access to relevant data (Bernhardt, 2005). Our case studies indicate that most principals felt quite uncertain about their understanding and use of numerical data for school improvement purposes as they began their work with the SLC. As one of our case study principals put it, "No one showed us how to analyze test scores before. They just told us to analyze test scores" (personal correspondence, 2005). And after their SLC experiences, most became highly data driven in their decision making, in the process transforming their schools into data-driven organizations.

While the demand for data-driven decision making on the part of school leaders is ubiquitous, the opportunities for suitable capacity development is not. A leadership center can contribute significantly to the data-driven nature of principals' decisions—and their feelings of efficacy about this aspect of their job—by organizing hands-on training to build capacity. This was a core feature not only of the later SLC summer institutes, but eventually of follow up workshops as well. These initiatives focused primarily on the achievement data collected by the state—how to interpret such evidence and make productive use of it in setting school improvement priorities.

Using the SLC as an example, it also seems clear that a leadership center can contribute to data-driven decision making by actually locating data relevant to the much broader array of policy decisions with which schools are faced, at the request of schools. This is a function performed by SLC's Research Services and has served to greatly enhance the use of research evidence for improving practice. Noteworthy here is the encouragement of the use of relevant research in all phases of the school improvement process. Participation in SLC-LI taught fellows to use data and connect to available research in identifying problems, analyzing their causes, developing action plans, and evaluating the implementation of these plans.

Lesson Six: Practice What You Preach (and Be Nice)

We know that teachers' treatment of students is often influenced by how administrators treat teachers. Being the object of respectful behavior inclines the recipient to treat others in a similarly respectful manner.

One of the lessons from our 12 cases is the remarkable influence on principals' relations with their staffs and students from the treatment the principals received from SLC staff. Becoming an SLC fellow was to instantly enjoy the high regard of SLC staff. Your experiences were validated. Your ideas were listened to. Your successes were celebrated. Your challenges were appreciated. SLC staff modeled, in their relationships with fellows, the meaning of transformative leadership, the value of shared decision making, a commitment to evidence-based practice, and an openness to continuous learning. The principals in our 12 case studies noticed. As one remarked, "SLC has been a real bright spot in my life as a principal . . . it is rare [for principals] to be treated as the respected leaders of their business" (personal correspondence, 2005).

In fact, for several of them, the SLC example may have been a more powerful influence than the explicit training provided by SLC.

Lesson Seven: A Little Bit of Money Goes a Long Way

We have long known that small amounts of discretionary money can have disproportionate consequences for school improvement (Louis & Miles, 1990). Such extra money not only has quite practical uses, it also symbolizes the importance the source of funding attaches to the work being funded, rewards people for initiative, and encourages greater effort and commitment.

SLC provided financial grants ranging from $5,000 to $15,000 to fellows' schools to help with school improvement. While this is a tiny proportion of a school's total budget, it may be a huge proportion of the funds available to a school for discretionary activity. In the 12 case schools, the money was used for new teaching materials, time for school improvement planning, and the like—not what one would imagine to be "discretionary" activity in a highly functioning organization in a perfect world. But these schools—and many others across the world—don't find themselves in anything close to a perfect world. Helping find, or helping teach schools how to find, discretionary money is a very useful focus for the work of a leadership center for principals and their staffs.

Lesson Eight: For a Long-Term Impact, Build a Community of Leaders

Efforts by a leadership center like the SLC to create a culture of cooperation among participants in its programs can have far-reaching, positive effects. SLC's attention to mentoring, partnering, and fostering communication among participants resulted in a "networked learning community" of principals extending well beyond the boundaries of their individual districts. One of our case study principals cited as most helpful to her the opportunity to be with other principals, to see that many of their struggles were no different from hers, regardless of differences in schools. She explained that the SLC stresses the importance of networking and the power of conversation to "help sustain, encourage, and support us. They help us celebrate when good things happen and lift us up when bad things happen" (personal correspondence, 2005). Members of this SLC-nurtured community now have access to extensive peer consultation, a menu of practical improvement strategies, and a valuable source of social support in a job that often seems isolated and underappreciated.

The advantages of participation in a community of principal-colleagues, as reflected in the 12 cases, overlap in large measure with the benefits of productive mentoring relationships reflected in research on this theme, for example: increased confidence and self-esteem, reduction in stress and frustration, practical advice and assistance, links to additional resources, a sounding board for new ideas, and improved communication skills (for a recent review of evidence, see Hobson & Sharp, 2005).

But the SLC learned, through hard experience, that networks of peers were far more acceptable to experienced school administrators than were mentoring relationships. Networks of peers provide equal-status access to many sources of advice rather than differentiated-status access to only one other source of advice. While mentoring may well be valuable for aspiring or novice school leaders, as Hobson and Sharp (2005) suggest, access to a peer network seems more helpful to experienced leaders.

Lesson Nine: Use the Community of Leaders to Retain Successful Leaders

While attrition in the principal ranks is endemic in the country at this time (e.g., see Whitaker, 2003), members of the networked learning communities created by the SLC and reflected in the 12 cases remain committed to their jobs and enthusiastic about what they are accomplishing. Building these communities through the work of leadership centers like the SLC may be one of the most promising responses in sight to the attrition problem. Most leadership centers should seriously consider including such network building as a key part of their overall mission.

How can centers do this community building? The sense of being valued and supported in their work, which principals developed through their SLC experiences, was a product of many initiatives, not all of which can be connected to school improvement work with a straight line. Consider, for example, the location of summer institutes in resort settings, the sincere and overt respect of fellows demonstrated by SLC staff, the regular social events hosted by the Center, the affirming and inspirational tone of many of Brian's (SLC's CEO) *Monday Messages,*[1] the inviting physical atmosphere of

---

1. He actually sends one out by e-mail *every* week with only a very short interruption around hurricane Katrina.

the Center's offices, and the attention paid to the work of individual principals and schools by Glenn (an SLC staff member).

None of this had been part of our case study principals' experiences in the other contexts of their professional lives. And none of these things added directly to the skills and knowledge they required for their school improvement efforts. But all of them helped to build the determination, persistence, and commitment principals needed to be successful at improving their schools. These initiatives also helped principals develop a perspective on the value of their work that continued to make the job an exciting one for them.

Lesson Ten: Use Inspiring Leadership Models to Recruit New Leaders

As we mentioned in our introduction, there is a distinct lack of interest among teachers in aspiring to the principalship as a career goal at the present time (Education Research Service, 2000). In contrast, an important feature of each of the 12 school cases was the development of teacher leadership and, in most cases, the adoption by these new teacher leaders of the principalship as a career goal for themselves.

While low administrator salaries, along with challenging working conditions, accounts for the widespread lack of interest in school administration, perhaps the most influential factor is teachers' perceptions of what it means to be a principal (e.g., see Sandham, 2001). Too many principals provide an uninspiring model of the principalship to their teachers. But when a leadership center dramatically alters a principal's style of leadership from one that is autocratic, perhaps not well informed, and based on positional power, to one that is more democratic, data driven, and consensual, teachers experience a role that many find attractive. Our 12 cases illustrate just how powerful this effect can be.

In concert with lesson eight, then, the justification for the work of leadership centers needs to be viewed more broadly than only leading to school improvement and increased student learning. While these are obviously central and necessary goals for leadership centers, in the current administrator recruitment and retention context, they are not sufficient. Leadership centers are in a powerful position to improve administrator recruitment and retention across the country and should explicitly aim to do so.

CONCLUSION

So, this is what we have learned to this point. By promoting relational trust (Bryk & Schneider, 2002) and modeling the attributes of a learning organization, the SLC has been able to foster the creation of a culture of learning essential to the development of school leaders who take on the challenging puzzles associated with improving schools. Indeed, the SLC was founded on the belief that sound relationships must be built first—or early—and only then will individual leaders engage in the kind of transformational activities needed to promote change within their schools.

At the outset, the team that designed the SLC wrestled with how to develop (and model) such courageous leadership. The Center and its staff model many practices that improve the chances of success for school leaders: shared decision making through, for example, the creation of structures to involve fellows; risk taking through the development of new programs and practices; and the importance of continuous evaluation through the Center's own evaluation practices. The stability of the Center; its focus on facilitative processes for school improvement; its balance of programming that empowers and develops individuals, teams, and networks; and the connectedness promoted through Center activities promotes the development of confidence among otherwise isolated professionals to be courageous leaders.

"What about the transferability of the SLC initiatives and the lessons we have drawn from our experiences?" you might be asking at this point. Much of what the SLC accomplishes, we want to emphasize, is by design. It is the product of a conscious effort by staff, the board, the evaluator, and the fellows themselves. Key to our design, for example, was commitment to a mission that makes "courageous leadership for school improvement" the focus; having a full-time staff, which makes it possible to devote the time and energy needed to continuously discuss and examine programs and practices; to incorporate feedback from fellows; to nurture the network among fellows; and otherwise act as steward of the mission; devoting resources to the external evaluation; and establishing a relationship with the evaluator or evaluators as a critical friend.

Creating a culture, as we have described it, has been vitally important for the SLC. In large part, however, SLC structures make this possible. Staff spent enormous amounts of time and energy in meetings making this explicit to one another. Furthermore, those facing the task of creating a leadership program need to understand that it just does not happen by chance. Like any other complex change effort, the SLC program was not all planned at the outset. The program that developed over time was the product of extensive discussions about the kind of leadership SLC staff wanted to model—risk taking, dealing with ambiguity, using available research, actively encouraging and using feedback, and the like.

Sustaining the energy, commitment, and enthusiasm of school leaders goes hand in hand with improving their capacities. Those responsible for this task might well be advised to think of capacity development as their primary goal, but one pursued in a way that also sustains school leaders' positive dispositions toward their work and continued willingness to do the heavy lifting we should all be grateful they are willing to do.

References

Bernhardt, V., (2005). Data tools for school improvement, *Educational Leadership, 62*(5), 66–69.

Bryk, A., & Schneider, B. (2002). *Trust in schools: A core resource for improvement.* New York: Russell Sage Foundation.

Chrispeels, J. H. (2004). Sharing leadership: Learning from challenge—aiming toward promise. In J. H. Chrispeels (Ed.), *Learning to lead together: The promise and challenge of sharing leadership* (pp. 363–376). Thousand Oaks, CA: Sage.

Earl, L., & Katz, S. (2002). Leading schools in a data-rich world. In K. Leithwood & P. Hallinger (Eds.), *Second International Handbook of Educational Leadership and Administration* (Vol. 8). Dordrect, The Netherlands: Kluwer.

Education Research Service, National Association of Elementary School Principals, & National Association of Secondary School Principals. (2000). *The principal, keystone of a high-achieving school: Attracting and keeping the leaders we need.* Arlington, VA: Author.

Frost, D., & Durrant, J. (2004). Supporting teachers' leadership: What can principals do? A teachers' perspective from research. In J. H. Chrispeels (Ed.), *Learning to lead together: The promise and challenge of sharing leadership* (pp. 307–326). Thousand Oaks, CA: Sage.

Harvard Education Letter. (2000, January/February). Retrieved February 20, 2009, from http://www.edletter.org/past/issues/2000-jf/grades.shtml

Hobson, A. J., & Sharp, C. (2005). Head to head: A systematic review of the research evidence on mentoring new head teachers. *School Leadership and Management, 25*(1), 25–42.

Lambert, L., (2005). Leadership for lasting reform. *Educational Leadership, 62*(5), 62–65.

Leithwood, K., Riedlinger, B., Bauer, S., & Jantzi, D. (2003). Leadership program effects on student learning: The case of the Greater New Orleans School Leadership Center. *Journal of School Leadership and Management, 13*(6), 707–738.

Linn, R. (2003). Accountability: Responsibility and reasonable expectations. *Educational Researcher, 32*(7), 3–13.

Louis, K., & Miles, M. B. (1990). *Improving the urban high school: What works and why.* New York: Teachers College Press.

Malone, B., Sharp, W., & Walter, J. (2001). *What's right about the principalship.* Paper presented at the annual meeting of the Mid-Western Educational Research Association, Chicago, IL.

Menter, I., Hollingan, C., & Mthenjwa, V. (2005). Reaching the parts that need to be reached? The impact of the Scottish Qualification for Headship. *School Leadership and Management, 25*(1), 7–23.

Peterson, K. D. (2001). *The professional development of principals: Innovations and opportunities.* Paper presented at the first meeting of the National Commission for the Advancement of Educational Leadership Preparation. Rancine, WI.

Sandham, J. L. (2001, April 4). California faces a shortage of administrators, report warns. *Education Week, 20*(29), 5.

Sparks, D., & Hirsh, S. (2000). *Learning to lead, leading to learn.* Oxford, OH: National Staff Development Council.

Swaffield, S. (2005). No sleeping partners: Relationships between head teachers and critical friends. *School Leadership and Management, 25*(1), 43–57.

Whitaker, K. S. (2003). Superintendent perceptions of quantity and quality of principal candidates. *Journal of School Leadership, 13*(2), 159–180.

Wikeley, F., Stoll, L., Murillo, J., & De Jong, R. (2005). Evaluating effective school improvement: Case studies of programmes in eight European countries and their contribution to the effective school improvement model. *School Effectiveness and School Improvement, 16*(4), 387–406.

PART III

District-Level Change

Michael Fullan

Schools, as a group, cannot move forward unless the district is part of the solution. The district is a crucial part of the infrastructure with respect to leadership development, capacity building, mobilization and use of data, and intervention.

The article by Fullan and Sharratt depicts one district's journey into sustaining leadership: York Region, a large multicultural district just north of Toronto has stayed the course in changing the culture of the district and its 190 schools.

Childress and her colleagues at Harvard similarly have developed a compelling district-wide "coherence framework" with an instructional core surrounded by a set of strategies, structures, and resources required for district capacity building aimed at student learning and achievement.

There is no doubt that the role of the district in many jurisdictions is being recast along the line of the growing knowledge about multilevel reform. Once again, it is neither top-down nor bottom-up that works but rather a coordinated partnership between the two levels.

CHAPTER ELEVEN

Sustaining Leadership in Complex Times

An Individual and System Solution

Michael Fullan

Lyn Sharratt

INTRODUCTION

Leadership energy has recently received greater attention as people grapple with the complexity, not only of achieving substantial improvement under challenging circumstances, but also of maintaining organizational momentum for continuous improvement (see Davies, 2005; Fullan, 2005, 2006; Fullan, Hill, & Crévola, 2006; Hargreaves & Fink, 2006; Loehr & Schwartz, 2003).

In this chapter, we delve into the issues of leadership sustainability by examining a large school district with which we are associated. It is a particularly appropriate case for the topic, because the district has been intensively engaged in a district-wide reform for the past five years and has relied heavily on mobilizing leadership at all levels of the system. The question of interest is "Under what conditions can leaders in the system sustain their efforts individually and collectively?"

We first provide some context in describing the district and the Literacy Collaborative (LC) model that has been the focus of reform. Second, we present the results up to this point. Third, we get into the substance of sustainability by drawing directly on data from school principals in the district. Finally, we take up the implications for sustaining leadership presence as a continuous force for improvement, concluding that it is both an individual and a system responsibility. We note that if the latter two elements can operate in an interdependent manner, the conditions for leadership energy, continuous renewal, and sustainability have a greater chance of becoming embedded.

DISTRICT CONTEXT

York Region District School Board (YRDSB) is a large multicultural district just north of Toronto, Ontario, Canada. It is rapidly growing with a diverse sociocultural and linguistic population with over 100 different languages spoken in their schools. On average, the school board has been opening 5 elementary schools a year for the last five years and a secondary school every other year. There are a total of 140 elementary schools and 27 secondary schools with over 108,000 students and 8,000 teachers.

In 2000, when the district began its student achievement improvement strategy in earnest, director of education, Bill Hogarth, set out to develop the best possible model for reform, drawing heavily on external ideas but developing a capacity from within the district to lead the reform with a critical mass of leaders at all levels of the district. The district decided the foundation for improving student achievement was to focus on improving literacy through a model that came to be known as the Literacy Collaborative. Key features of the approach included

- Articulating a clear vision and commitment to a system literacy priority for all students, which is continually communicated to everyone in the system
- Developing a system-wide comprehensive plan and framework for continuous improvement (SPCI)
- Using data to drive instruction and determine resources

- Building administrator and teacher capacity to teach literacy for all students
- Establishing professional learning communities at all levels of the system and beyond the district

The district developed a strong team of curriculum coordinators and consultants, all focused on facilitating balanced literacy instruction. It also linked into external research development expertise, particularly with the Ontario Institute for Studies in Education of the University of Toronto (OISE/UT). Assessment of the effectiveness of the implementation was evaluated annually. Capacity building focused on literacy assessment for learning, instructional strategies, and on change management. In this case, *capacity building* means any strategy that develops the collective efficacy of a group to raise the bar and close the gap of student achievement through (1) new knowledge competencies and skills, (2) enhanced resources, and (3) greater motivation. The operative word is *collective*—what the group can do whether it is a given school or, indeed, the whole district to raise the bar and close the gap of student achievement.

The district has invested in ongoing, systematic professional development in literacy, assessment literacy, knowledge of the learner, instructional intelligence and e-learning, as well as professional learning focusing on change knowledge (understanding the change process, dealing with resistance, building professional learning communities, leadership and facilitation skills, and the like). The full-blown model is shown in Figure 11.1.

The model may appear overwhelming, and we do not intend to explain it in detail here. In fact, the model was developed over time and is presented and discussed on an ongoing basis within the system to clarify the overall vision and to continuously improve the approach. Our point here is that the model is explicit, evolutionary (open to refinement based on ongoing evidence), and comprehensive. It reflects and guides the work of the district and is used by instructional leaders at all levels of the system.

More specifically, the LC model involved developing and supporting school literacy teams, starting with an initial cohort in 2001/2002 and adding schools over a four-year period until all schools in the district were involved, elementary and secondary. Each school team consisted of three people—the principal, the

Figure 11.1 The Literacy Collaborative Vision

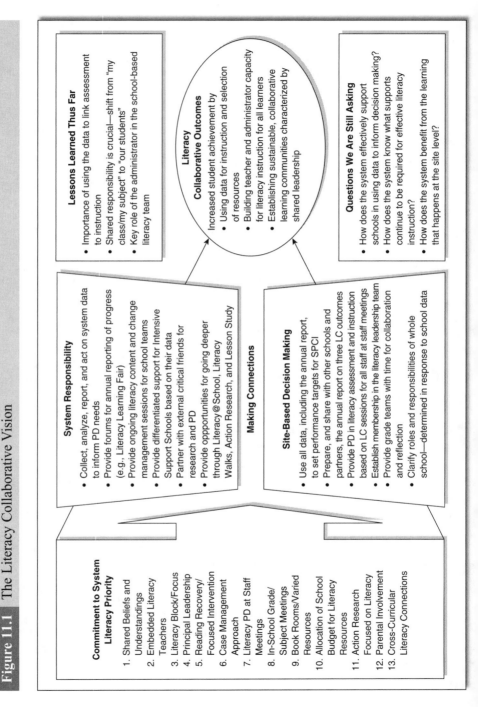

Commitment to System Literacy Priority

1. Shared Beliefs and Understandings
2. Embedded Literacy Teachers
3. Literacy Block/Focus
4. Principal Leadership
5. Reading Recovery/Focused Intervention
6. Case Management Approach
7. Literacy PD at Staff Meetings
8. In-School Grade/Subject Meetings
9. Book Rooms/Varied Resources
10. Allocation of School Budget for Literacy Resources
11. Action Research Focused on Literacy
12. Parental Involvement
13. Cross-Curricular Literacy Connections

System Responsibility

- Collect, analyze, report, and act on system data to inform PD needs
- Provide forums for annual reporting of progress (e.g., Literacy Learning Fair)
- Provide ongoing literacy content and change management sessions for school teams
- Provide differentiated support for Intensive Support Schools based on their data
- Partner with external critical friends for research and PD
- Provide opportunities for going deeper through Literacy@School, Literacy Walks, Action Research, and Lesson Study

Making Connections

Site-Based Decision Making

- Use all data, including the annual report, to set performance targets for SPCI
- Prepare, and share with other schools and partners, the annual report on three LC outcomes
- Provide PD in literacy assessment and instruction based on LC sessions for all staff at staff meetings
- Establish membership in the literacy leadership team
- Provide grade teams with time for collaboration and reflection
- Clarify roles and responsibilities of whole school—determined in response to school data

Lessons Learned Thus Far

- Importance of using the data to link assessment to instruction
- Shared responsibility is crucial—shift from "my class/my subject" to "our students"
- Key role of the administrator in the school-based literacy team

Literacy Collaborative Outcomes

Increased student achievement by

- Using data for instruction and selection of resources
- Building teacher and administrator capacity for literacy instruction for all learners
- Establishing sustainable, collaborative learning communities characterized by shared leadership

Questions We Are Still Asking

- How does the system effectively support schools in using data to inform decision making?
- How does the system know what supports continue to be required for effective literacy instruction?
- How does the system benefit from the learning that happens at the site level?

literacy teacher (a leadership role typically released for .25 to .5 time to work alongside the principal and classroom teachers during the school day), and the special education resource teacher (SERT). (Note: the funding of the literacy teacher is from the school district's staffing, using the existing budget, and is not supported by provincial educational funding.) The teams committed to participating in regional literacy professional development (PD) once a month and in change management sessions, led by Carol Rolheiser and Michael Fullan (OISE/UT), four times a year.

The cohorts joined LC, starting with the most disadvantaged elementary schools. In 2001/2002, 17 elementary schools formed the first cohort; 21 schools were added in 2002/2003; 45 in 2003/2004, and the remaining 57 schools joined in 2004/2005. Thus, by 2005, all schools were involved, including all 27 secondary schools. There is a longstanding saying in the change literature that "change is a process, not an event." Such a process was actualized in York Region District School Board, not just because the professional development sessions were continuous over multiple years but also because the strategy required school teams, working with their staffs, to apply ideas in between sessions and to continually build them into everyday practice. It was what happened in the schools in between sessions that counted. Ideas were constantly applied and discussed as the district emphasized "learning in context," that is, learning by applying new ideas, building on them, and being reenergized by the successes achieved.

In short, the model was based on best knowledge. Comprehensive in coverage, the model was constantly shared and refined with all stakeholders—the school teams, the curriculum coordinator and consultant staff, the community, school board trustees, and the system as a whole. Moreover, there was a multiyear commitment funded at the board table and outlined in a comprehensive system plan for continuous improvement (SPCI) so that the district stayed on course with the strategy. There was no mistaking that LC was clearly the system priority.

Each June, the district organizes a Literacy Learning Fair in which the literacy leadership teams from *all* schools present what they have accomplished and learned. Schools must report on the three goals of LC: to increase students' literacy achievement by

- Using data to drive instruction and to select appropriate literacy resources

- Building administrators' and teachers' capacity for successful literacy instruction
- Establishing professional learning communities across the district

The Literacy Learning Fair is part celebration, part peer pressure, and part peer support to keep reaching new levels of achievement. By annually sharing every schools' commitment to and accomplishment of increased student achievement, the 400 participants contributed to organization and individual leadership energy renewal.

RESULTS SO FAR

The intent here is not to explain the results in detail, but rather but to convey enough detail that it is clear that YRDSB is a district on the move (see Sharratt and Fullan, 2005, for a more in-depth analysis of results). Our main question of interest in this chapter is, what are the issues in *sustaining* improvement—what are the key leadership issues for the immediate future in a system that is already highly focused and intentional?

Assessment of student achievement in reading, writing, and mathematics for third-grade and sixth-grade children is conducted annually by the Education Quality and Accountability Office (EQAO). The EQAO is an arm's-length government agency charged with assessing all students in the province and communicating the results. To take third-grade writing as an example, over the past five years (from 1999–2000 to 2004–2005), York has moved from 66% of the students reaching the provincial standard to approximately 75%. During the first three years of this period, the province as a whole was flat-lined at around 55% until it launched in 2003 a province-wide strategy much along the lines of York's capacity-building but applied to all 72 districts in the province—latterly the province has moved from 55% to 63% (see Fullan, 2006). Table 11.1 describes these quantitative results in more detail.

The aggregate figures mask the more fine-grained explanation of how results were achieved in specific schools. In Sharratt and Fullan (2006), we present data that show that those schools that had principal and teacher-leadership that focused more specifically on

Table 11.1	Five-Year Span in EQAO Results in YRDSB, 1999–2005		
EQAO (Method 2)	1999 (Baseline Year Before District's Literacy Focus)	2005	% Increase
Grade 3 Reading	59	69	10
Grade 3 Writing	66	75	9
Grade 3 Mathematics	70	80	10
Grade 6 Reading	61	75	14
Grade 6 Writing	59	72	13
Grade 6 Mathematics	63	76	13
% ESL/ELD	Gr. 3, 4	11	7
Learners	Gr. 6, 4	6	2
ESL/ELD Grade 3 Reading	34	56	22
ESL/ELD Grade 3 Writing	47	69	22
ESL/ELD Grade 3 Mathematics	62	75	13
ESL/ELD Grade 6 Reading	27	53	26
ESL/ELD Grade 6 Writing	27	62	35
ESL/ELD Grade 6 Mathematics	62	74	12
OSSLT (diploma bearing assessment)	Oct. 2002, 77%	Oct. 2004, 87%	10
Reading at the end of Grade 1 (Reading Recovery site reports)	59%	83%	24

SOURCE: Sharratt & Rolheiser, 2006

all 13 parameters of the LC model in action achieved much greater results, including many of the most disadvantaged schools that began much below the YRDSB and the Ontario average, only to surpass both averages over the ensuing five years. As we said in our earlier paper, the leadership teams in these schools

- Clearly understood the model and most important lived the shared beliefs and understandings
- Did continuous self-assessment, striving to align behavior and beliefs among the principal, teacher-leaders, and staff as a whole
- Did not let other "distractors" divert their focus and energy. In fact, they drew or renewed their leadership energy by means of understanding their improvement

There are many schools in York Region that have these qualities and the system is now working toward greater consistency. For example, 28 elementary and 6 secondary schools were identified, using data, as "stuck" or declining and in 2005/2006 are receiving more intensive capacity-building support for school leadership teams from the curriculum and instructional services team (in the meantime, *all* schools in York Region continue to be engaged in district-wide reform, including all 27 secondary schools).

There is little doubt that there is widespread support for and understanding of LC in the district. In April 2005, we conducted a survey of all school teams in the district (each school leadership team consists of the principal, the lead literacy teacher, and the special education resource teacher). We received 387, or a 76%, return. The results from the survey showed that a very high percentage of school leaders perceived that LC had a strong, positive impact. The percentage scoring 4 or 5 on a five-point impact scale for selected questions is displayed in Table 11.2.

Granted that this survey does not tap into the perceptions of individual teachers but the leadership teams are very much in close interaction with classroom teachers, we conclude that it is accurate to say that the system as a whole has been energized by the strategy and the strong results being obtained. We get further confirmation from the fact that the provincial Literacy Numeracy Secretariat identified YRDSB as one of eight school districts that exemplified quality strategies in action. But our interest in this chapter is not about the results so far. Rather, what are the prospects for sustainability? How

Table 11.2	The Literacy Collaborative Has . . .	
1. Provided teachers with a wider range of teaching strategies		90%
2. Helped ensure adequate resources to support students		78%
3. Raised the expertise of teachers within their schools		88%
4. Increased the school-wide focus on literacy		95%
5. Clarified the role of all teachers in the support of literacy		78%
6. Provided more attention and assistance to students at risk		83%
7. Raised literacy expectations for all students		90%
8. Produced more consistency and continuity in literacy across subjects		75%
9. Fostered a more positive attitude among staff regarding literacy teaching		85%
10. Facilitated sharing of expertise with teachers from other schools		69%

do individual principals sustain their commitment? How can the system help? Could it be that large-scale initiatives, even if successful, eventually take their toll and lead to diminished effort in light of relentless demands?

THE NATURE AND PROSPECTS OF SUSTAINABILITY

Hargreaves and Fink (2006) define sustainability in this way: "Sustainability does not simply mean whether something will last. It addresses how particular initiatives can be developed without compromising the development of others in the environment now or in the future" (p. 30). Thus, intentional reform models, like LC, must unfold in a way that all schools will benefit. The spirit underlying such approaches attempts to create a we-we mindset. As a result of purposeful interaction within and across schools, school leaders become more aware of, and indeed more committed to, the success of other schools in addition to their own.

It is our contention in this chapter that while individual leaders can and must work on their own sustaining energies, the conditions for sustaining large numbers of people can only be fostered if the organization as a whole is working in this direction. Moreover, we maintain that focusing on sustainability must become more deliberate and precise. It needs explicit attention—it must be worked on in a self- and organizationally conscious manner.

This position is reinforced by the findings of two of the more informative books on organizational change, which confirm the basic conditions for sustainability. Jim Collins (2001), in his well-known book, *Good to Great,* compares Fortune 500 companies that had "good" performance with those that had "great" performance as measured by 15 or more years of continuous financial success. Collins and his colleagues found five key themes associated with ongoing success. The first three, he claims, are more important early on because they build momentum. First, he found that we need more "executive leaders" who can help build enduring greatness (leaders whose main mark is not only their contribution to success but also relative to how many leaders they leave behind who can go even further). Second, he emphasizes that organizations need to work on securing "who," not just "what." The "who," in this case, are leaders who can help develop the five themes in question. The third theme is "confront the brutal facts," that is, a relentless focus on examining data for making improvements. The fourth theme was the "hedgehog effect"—a hedgehog is an animal that once it focuses is hard to distract. Thus, sustainable organizations learn to concentrate through passion, expertise, and mobilization of resources in a way that keeps them going. The fifth theme is "disciplined inquiry"—always problem solving in relation to the central mission. Collins calls the overall effect the "flywheel." This is clearly related to sustainability because it takes less energy to keep the flywheel going once it is under way, permitting leaders to go deeper, which leads to greater success. More recently, Collins (2005) has confirmed that these ideas apply to the social sector, not because they come from business, but because they focus on getting and maintaining greatness. The virtuous circle builds and further attracts believers and resources by getting and leveraging results.

An identical finding is contained in Kanter's (2004) study of *Confidence: How Winning and Losing Streaks Begin and End.* "Confidence," says Kanter, "influences the willingness to invest—to commit money, time, reputation, emotional energy, or other resources—or withhold or hedge investments" (p. 7). Kanter's solution is framed around developing three interconnected cornerstones—accountability, collaboration, and initiative. It is these conditions that generate sustaining investments of energy and commitment.

The system must also foster what we have come to call "positive pressure" (Fullan, 2006). A positive pressure is one that is non-pejorative, that assumes that capacity is at the root of success, and that focused capacity-building strategies promote transparency in sharing practices and viewing results. In other words, one key to getting at sustainability is to bring issues out into the open in order to understand them and, in turn, in order to address any problems.

In sum, the key concepts for us pertain to whether the system goes about its work in a way that helps people focus, that motivates and energizes people to make investments that are sensitive to the ebb and flow of energies, that uses success to beget more success, and that creates a critical mass of leaders who work together on these very matters.

Sustainability in York Region

There are very little direct data available in the literature on what leaders in given systems think about in relation to the concept of sustainability. We decided, then, that a good place to start would be to go to the source and ask YRDSB principals three questions:

1. How do you, as leader, sustain your school's literacy initiative?

2. How do you maintain energy and renewal for your staff to sustain the literacy focus?

3. How do you maintain your energy and renewal for yourself to sustain the literacy focus?

We set out to select a large number of principals on the basis of how active they were in the LC. Thus, this is not a random sample but one in which the leaders identified were engaged in the reform. We wanted to know what active, purposeful principals thought about sustainability. We did not, it should be noted, select on a narrow basis a few exceptionally active principals. We wanted the sample to represent typical principals who could reflect what happens when "regular" principals get immersed in ongoing change. We identified 61 elementary and 18 secondary school principals and asked them to respond in writing to the three questions. The response was overwhelming with 50 (82%) of the elementary and 17 (94%) of the secondary principals responding. This is admittedly a selective sample but is large and diverse, representing about 38% of the total in the district. We found, as expected, that, although the questions were open-ended, the vast majority of responses related to the components of the LC model. In other words, given that the model was intended to mobilize support at the school level for a sustained focus on literacy, and given that the model was developed in close communication with principals, we would expect that school leaders would gravitate to the content of the strategy when they thought (unprompted) about sustainability. We report below on the main themes that respondents spontaneously formulated, indicating the percentage of those who commented on the theme along with a representative quote or two relevant to the topic. Our interest here is in identifying the conditions or elements that are conducive to sustaining focus and energy on continuous improvement. Think of sustainability conditions as those that motivate people to continue to invest their energies in working with others to accomplish greater improvement.

Question 1: How do you, as leader, sustain your school's literacy initiative?

There were five major themes that attracted high numbers of comments:

1. Shared beliefs, goals, and vision

2. Distributed leadership and professional learning cultures

3. Data-based decisions/impact measures/celebrating success

4. Resources

5. School-community/home relations

As we have found before, these are recurring themes (Sharratt, 2001); however, they are found here to be even more precise. We also note that shared beliefs is more of an outcome of a quality process than a precondition (Fullan, 2006). Put differently, one condition for sustainability involves working on defining, shaping, and refining the shared vision of the school—in this case, using school data in relation to literacy improvement. The more that beliefs are shared, the greater the ongoing effort and the efficiency of the effort. Over 60% of respondents identified shared beliefs, as in the following three comments:

> A common goal of improved student achievement and the attitude that all students can learn is embedded in the culture of the school.

> To sustain the school's literacy implementation, we try to maintain focus and assure that we have a common language. We try to set a few clear targets, and we have an overall vision regarding where we want our students to be across the grades.

> When we reflect on the impact of our instructional decisions and what the data tell us that students are learning, it creates "intellectual energy." It becomes a craving to impact the learning of every student.

A second key factor associated with continued success is what we have come to call the presence of dedicated "second change agents" or what is sometimes referred to as distributive leadership—a critical mass of leaders led by the principal working on establishing a culture of ongoing learning. The principal is the first change agent. Having one or more "second change agents" is crucial—for example, literacy lead teachers with direct responsibility and time during the school day to work with other teachers in their classrooms, to link teachers with each other internally and across schools, to help set up data management systems, and to work with principals on school improvement. Over 70% of respondents highlighted this aspect:

> Sustaining the momentum within the school is possible because of the many levels of support available to schools. The staffing made available for literacy coaches has been critical. This has given our school a teacher-leader who is working to increase the knowledge of those around her.

> We model processes and literacy content at staff meetings and build shared leadership by providing staff opportunities to take leadership roles in modeling and facilitating the use of

information gained at LC sessions. As a principal, I fully utilize the concept of sharing leadership and creating a learning community. The sharing of leadership allows the administrative team and me to pace ourselves in terms of energy expenditure.

Administration communicates clear expectations to staff about why/how/when literacy instruction and focus occur in classrooms. Ensure that staff members have the tools, skills, and so on to use effective literacy practices (i.e., no excuses).

Our primary learning team truly is a professional learning community with many teachers doing projects together and sharing ideas.

By using staff meetings, divisional meetings, and grade-partner planning times, teachers are encouraged to reflect on the needs of all students, generally, and students at risk specifically.

Third, data-driven instruction and the ubiquitous presence and use of data are core themes for promoting and maintaining effort. The case management approach is in place in all elementary schools where individual students are tracked, with corrective action taking place on an ongoing basis. Over 40% of responses related to this theme:

Student achievement in both literacy and numeracy is a focus for transition planning for students coming from eighth grade to ninth grade. We make particular note of student achievement levels in grades three and six EQAO assessments. (Secondary principal).

It was a natural step for us to [use case data] to strive for differentiated instruction to provide for the diverse needs in each classroom.

Success breeds success. What we have done to date has proved to make a difference to increased student achievement. We celebrate this!

We have set aside time to review school results—to identify areas of weakness and to share successful approaches.

Fourth, resources are part and parcel of continued success, provided that they are part of a cycle of success. Kick start the process with new resources, and then have success chase the money—this year's success is next year's additional resources (Fullan, 2006). Some 35% highlighted this factor:

We have invested heavily in book rooms and appropriate class-room libraries for all three divisions.

We carry out decisions about the school resources in the area of literacy based on our school plan for continuous improvement. We allocate our financial, human, and material resources in a way that makes literacy a priority.

The fifth theme for sustainability is probably one of the most important in the long run but also the most difficult to establish, namely, school-to-home community relationships. This element was reflected in comments from almost 40% of respondents.

We have extended our partnerships with the parents and guardians from day one. This community has extended our understanding of cultural diversity—English as a second language and economic and lifestyle impact on children's learning.

Finally, a kind of omnibus comment struck us as a particularly apropos summary with respect to Question 1:

Support and encouragement are crucial. Pushing too hard never works. Magic happens when teachers take initiative within a framework that has been developed by the district. Incorporating PD into staff and division meetings needs to be led by staff, not the principal. When teachers share their best practices, things happen. Providing both time and resources for mentoring and team teaching ensures that literacy becomes and remains a focus. Walking the fine line between push and pull is always an exciting challenge and worth the time to build strong leaders in a school.

Question 2: How do you maintain energy and renewal for your staff to sustain the literacy focus?

Our second question extended the school sustainability question more directly to focus on staff. As expected, there was overlap with the first question but more personally based aspects surfaced. We can use the same five categories to capture the comments.

First, with respect to shared beliefs, about 30% of the responses related to this category:

I have very high expectations for myself and others. I expect the best and then offer opportunities and experiences to help others improve.

Time to focus on the goals of the school as a team has been met in an improved way this year and is making a difference.

Talk about buy in—we all have a common message, and again it gets linked back to that common vision.

Second, for leadership and learning cultures, principals talked about the day-to-day built-in support for what we call "learning in context"—the kind of learning that occurs every day because it becomes part of the culture. About 45% to 60% (depending on the subcategory) responded along these lines:

Teacher mentoring and team teaching have been important methods used to sustain the literacy implementation and energy in such a large school.

The literacy teachers (literacy coaches) have given staff many opportunities for support and role modeling. We give teachers time to collaborate with their grade partners.

Staff members need time to hear about a concept, learn about it, experiment with it, work it into everyday practice, consolidate it, and ultimately sustain it as part of good teaching practice.

Probably the most effective means for sustaining something is the teachers' own enthusiasm when they see their students progressing and responding to strategies they are using. It's catching!

A culture of shared leadership is in place. We promote shared leadership in the school, and teachers feel comfortable assuming these roles.

The external training provided by the district based on the LC model is a great motivator for me. I always bring back little seeds that I plant back at the school.

The opportunities available through the LC have been excellent, and the increased opportunities for more teachers attending workshops have provided great motivation and excitement at every level of the school.

Third, the use of data on student achievement as a tool for improvement, playing itself out in a learning culture, is crucial for maintaining focus and momentum was mentioned directly by 20% of the respondents and by many more in relation to establishing sharing cultures:

We analyzed the data collected, charted the students identified as "at risk" in the fall, and made plans to address their needs.

Our staff meeting agenda-planning focus is on student data and related improvement ideas and activities, while keeping operational and informational items to an absolute minimum!

Fourth, about 25% of the respondents mentioned resources:

Our book room is a central part of our school. Our teachers take tremendous ownership for it. They look forward to buying for it and keeping it up.

Budget for initiatives or simply having the resources in place is vital to ensuring that the change process is not interrupted or discarded and is integral to creating a culture of cohesiveness as staff members work and take ownership of literacy in their classrooms and in the school.

Timetabling, shared grade-level prep time, using curriculum instructional supply teacher days, and freeing up teachers to engage in professional learning are key to maintaining the focus.

Fifth, only a small minority (10%) mentioned home-school relations as a sustainer, possibly because this is the most difficult aspect and takes the longest to develop. In our experience, principals and teachers need to develop their own professional learning communities to a certain point first, before they reach out in a more proactive way to the community:

Key is engaging all educational partners and effectively using many volunteers, including cooperative education students, tutors in the classroom, and other community resources— human and nonhuman.

Question 3: How do you maintain your energy and renewal for yourself to sustain the literacy focus?

The third major question in this research is the most personal because it asks principals what they, themselves, do to maintain their own energy and renewal. Three interrelated clusters stood out:

1. Personal renewal and challenge
2. Passion expressed as student success (passion without success is a nonsustainer)
3. The social basis of sustainability

Over two thirds of respondents identified personal growth and stimulus as sustaining them:

> It may sound trite, but if we are asking our staff and students (and other employees) to read, read, read, then we had better be reading as well. I find that this is important in reminding me how important literacy is, so I read all the time, including professional reading, but more importantly, expanding to novels, newspapers, and so on.

> The personal satisfaction comes from learning new skills myself and participating in PD provided by the curriculum department.

> Ongoing learning opportunities through the LC, Literacy Walk training, in-school study groups, and personal professional reading are some of the vehicles for energizing and empowering the sustaining focus on literacy.

> Attending the LC sessions with the teachers is another way to maintain my energy and renewal.

> I endeavor to never let the mood of others or the stress felt by others determine my mood. I strive to be positive, professional, and set personal goals that I would like others to model.

The second theme was passion expressed through student success. Again, about two thirds spontaneously expressed this theme:

> But what really excites me is the children! Seeing their work displayed on the hallway walls, highlighting the reading comprehension strategy of the month, is very rewarding.

Watching amazing teachers work with students on something that you've taught them or that they have learned as a result of an opportunity that you have offered is energizing.

It is very easy to sustain the literacy focus when I see the positive results of the literacy practices our teachers implement in the school.

We focus on sharing and celebrating success that we're having. There is certainly an energy that comes from seeing that the instructional practices we are implementing are making a difference in the lives of all students.

Listening to success stories is encouraging and inspiring when one is occasionally faced with resistance or frustration.

The third theme—working on and appreciating personal well-being and the social nature of sustainability in and outside of school—was featured by, again, some 60% of the respondents:

My energy is sustained by watching and listening to dedicated staff that work hard and have fun doing it!

I spend time in classrooms to see literacy strategies in action (morning and afternoon walkthroughs).

I talk to staff, visit classrooms, and am aware of how staff members are maintaining a literacy focus in their classrooms on a daily basis.

Renewal comes when I spend time with my family and friends. This allows me to keep life in perspective, appreciate the little things, and not take myself too seriously.

I have learned to slow down (and that is hard for me) and digest the information from "above." I have learned how to prioritize the information and redistribute it to key staff for interpretation.

Finally, an overall comment seemed to capture the essence of personal sustainability:

I see literacy leadership as a never-ending cycle of learning and improvement. When you accept this idea, it becomes easier to accept personal renewal as an essential component of effective leadership.

IMPLICATIONS FOR SUSTAINABILITY

Our chapter is clearly only one snapshot, albeit of a large district that is taking leadership sustainability seriously. We think that the personal perspectives of a large number of school leaders are both a unique and valuable contribution to our knowledge of personal perceptions on the question of sustainability. As we stand back and survey the overall LC model from the perspective of conditions that favor sustainability, four propositions stand out for us.

Proposition One: Sustainability is not about prolonging specific innovations, but rather it is about establishing the conditions for continuous student improvement.

Proposition Two: Sustainability is not possible unless school leaders and system leaders are working on the same agenda.

Proposition Three: Proposition Two notwithstanding, sustainability is not furthered by school and system leaders simply agreeing on the direction of the reform. Rather, agreement is continually tested and extended by leaders at both school and system levels putting pressure on each other. Sustainability is a two-way or multiway street.

Proposition Four: We have a fair idea about what makes for sustainability within one district under conditions of stable leadership over a five or more year period, but we still do not know how sustainability fares when district leadership changes or when state leadership changes direction.

We have been able to identify some of the main themes of sustainability. They amount to focus, consistency, and mutual reinforcement between the school and district levels, staying the course, and developing an attitude that continuity of good direction and of increased student achievement is paramount. We know sustainability, as in continuous effort and energy, is always vulnerable. We know that sustaining cultures require a lot of work to build and maintain, but can be destroyed quickly with different leadership and change in political conditions. Yet, by making what works explicit, and by enabling more and more leaders at all levels of the system to be aware of the conditions that energize themselves and those with whom they work, the chances for continued success are greatly enhanced. Our general conclusion is to make the notion of sustainability transparent—foster open and continuous dialogue about whether system and school-level discussions are focused and, thus, whether energy is flourishing. Finally, we do not see sustainability as linear. There are always ebbs and flows, a time to stand back and regroup, and so on. Sustainable organizations are more likely to see positive flow as cyclical and, thus, treat setbacks as temporary, and more likely, in turn, to find ways of reenergizing. Indeed, sustainable organizations do not experience and do not expect continued good fortune, but rather stay the course when things are not going well. Persistence and resilience are the hallmarks of individuals and organizations that are self-conscious and confident about their own capacities to win more than they lose and to create their own self-fulfilling prophecies.

In short, it is not so much that people need to believe that sustainability is possible, but more that the only way to move forward is to be "in the game"—to be engaged, seeking, and helping to produce other leaders who are similarly disposed.

REFERENCES

Collins, J. (2001). *Good to great.* New York: HarperCollins.

Collins, J. (2005). *Good to great and the social sectors: Why business thinking is not the answer.* New York: HarperCollins.

Davies, B. (Ed.). (2005). *The essentials of school leadership.* London: Paul Chapman.

Fullan, M. (2005). *Leadership and sustainability.* Thousand Oaks, CA: Corwin; Toronto: Ontario Principals' Council.

Fullan, M. (2006). *Turnaround leadership.* San Francisco, CA: Jossey-Bass; Toronto: Ontario Principals' Council.

Fullan, M., Hill, P., & Crévola, C. (2006). *Breakthrough.* Thousand Oaks, CA: Corwin; Toronto: Ontario Principals' Council.

Hargreaves, A., & Fink, D. (2006). *Sustainable leadership.* San Francisco, CA: Jossey-Bass.

Kanter, R. M. (2004). *Confidence: How winning and losing streaks begin and end.* New York: Crown Publishers.

Loehr, J., & Schwartz, T. (2003). *The power of full engagement.* New York: Free Press.

Sharratt, L. (2001). Making the most of accountability policies: Is there a role for the school district? *Orbit, 32*(1), 37–42.

Sharratt, L., & Fullan, M. (2005). *The school district that did the right things right.* Annenberg Institute for School Reform. Providence, RI: Brown University.

Sharratt, L., & Fullan, M. (2006). Accomplishing districtwide reform. *Journal of School Leadership, 16,* 583–595.

Sharratt, L., & Rolheiser, C. (2006). *Miracles in progress: System change and coherence.* Toronto, Ontario, Canada: York Region District School Board.

Chapter Twelve

The PELP
Coherence Framework

Stacey Childress

Richard F. Elmore

Allen Grossman

Susan Moore Johnson

Organizational coherence means that the various parts of a school district are designed so that they work in sync with one another to achieve district goals. This concept grew out of our work with the Public Education Leadership Project (PELP) at Harvard University, a collaboration among faculty members at Harvard's graduate schools of business and education in partnership with a network of urban school districts. Through this project, we identified five common managerial challenges that urban districts face as they seek to implement a strategy for improving performance:

1. Implementing the strategy effectively across schools with different characteristics

2. Redesigning the organization so that it supports the strategy

3. Developing and managing human capital to carry out the strategy

4. Allocating resources in alignment with the strategy

5. Using performance data for decision making, organizational learning, and accountability

The district leaders we talked with, however, tended to see each of the five challenges as a separate problem rather than as related parts of a larger problem or solution. For example, effectively developing teachers' skills involves using timely, detailed, student performance data to highlight areas where teachers need to change or improve their instructional techniques. Similarly, allocating resources in ways that are aligned with students' specific learning needs is essential to ensure that a strategy can be implemented in meaningful ways in different sorts of schools.

Rather than focusing our research and case writing on these separate challenges, we developed the PELP Coherence Framework (PCF) to help leaders recognize the interdependence of various aspects of their school district—its culture, systems and structures, resources, stakeholder relationships, and environment—and to understand how they reinforce one another to support the implementation of an improvement strategy. The framework helps leaders use organizational design, human capital management, resource allocation, and accountability and performance improvement systems in coherent ways so that they can implement their strategy. This book brings together more than 20 of the cases and readings we developed over four years to illustrate these ideas.

The framework has roots in what business has taught us about organizational alignment. However, that knowledge has been elaborated by what we know about reform in education. Throughout its development, the framework has been informed by our interactions with senior leaders of large urban districts who face unique managerial challenges because of the size and complexity of their school systems and often because of the poverty of the communities they serve as well. Putting a districtwide strategy into practice requires building a coherent organization that connects to teachers' work in classrooms and enables people at all levels to carry out their part of the strategy. The framework identifies the organizational elements critical to high performance and poses a series of diagnostic questions about each element, all in an effort to bring them into coherence with the strategy and with each other. The elements of the framework are the instructional core, strategy,

Figure 12.1   PELP Coherence Framework

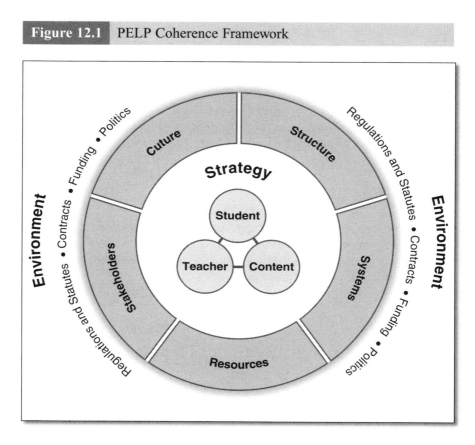

culture, structure, systems, resources, stakeholder relationships, and the environment.

STRATEGY AND THE INSTRUCTIONAL CORE

At the center of the framework is the instructional core, which represents the critical work of teaching and learning that goes on in classrooms. The core includes three interdependent components: teachers' knowledge and skill, students' engagement in their own learning, and academically challenging content. Surrounding the instructional core is strategy—the set of actions a district deliberately undertakes to strengthen the instructional core with the objective of increasing student learning and performance districtwide. In order to make teaching and learning more effective, a district's improvement strategy must articulate how it will strengthen and support the instructional core through integrated activities that increase teachers' knowledge and skill, change the students' role in the teaching and learning process, and ensure that curriculum is aligned with benchmarks for performance. However, *how* each district strengthens and supports the core may vary. In other words, two districts may design very different but equally effective strategies. The PELP Coherence Framework, rather than prescribing a particular strategy, asserts that organizational coherence at the district, school, and classroom levels will make a district's chosen approach more effective and sustainable.

Most other organizational decisions, resources, and activities should be directed toward supporting the district's strategy to make the core more powerful and effective. The other elements of the framework are aspects of the organization that must be brought into coherence with the strategy and each other.

CULTURE

Culture consists of the norms and behaviors in an organization; in other words, everyone's shared understanding of "how things work around here." Culture, whether strong or weak, does not change readily in response to edicts or slogans. Rather, it is reshaped gradually by changes in many individuals' practices and beliefs. When district leaders take specific actions, such as redefining roles or relationships, altering performance expectations, or using job assignments in creative ways, they send signals about which behaviors they value and desire throughout the organization. Over time, they can upend an entrenched counterproductive culture and see it replaced by a productive one.

The public education sector has long had a culture that valued effort—or the appearance of effort—more than results. As long as people seemed to be working hard, they could go about their business without being asked to work with colleagues or to be accountable for their students' performance. At its worst, this type of culture can lead to defeatism among teachers and administrators ("I taught it, but they didn't learn it"). In today's accountability environment, however, successful districts must develop a culture of collaboration, high expectations, and accountability throughout their schools.

STRUCTURE

Structure includes how people are organized, who has responsibility and accountability for results, and who makes or influences decisions. Districts usually develop their organizational structures haphazardly to support generation after generation of reform efforts, and then leave them in place long after the reform fad they were built for has passed from the scene. As a result, a district's structure often constrains rather than enables high performance and must be reinvented to support the implementation of an improvement strategy.

SYSTEMS

School districts manage themselves through a variety of important systems. In the same way that circulatory and nervous systems perform vital processes inside the skeletal structure of living organisms, an organization's systems provide the means by which important work flows through its structure. Some systems are formally designed by the district, while others emerge informally through practice. Whether formal or informal, the purpose of systems is to increase the district's efficiency and effectiveness in implementing strategy.

Systems are built around such important functions as career development and promotion, compensation, student assignment, resource allocation, organizational learning, and measurement and accountability. Effective systems are evenhanded and efficient, eliminating the need for individuals to "reinvent the wheel" or "know the right people" to get important things done.

RESOURCES

Money is usually the first thing leaders think about when resources are mentioned, and money is obviously important. But organizational resources also include people, time, and other assets such as technology and data. District leaders must allocate the full range of resources in ways that are coherent with the district's strategy if it is to be implemented effectively. This means being disciplined about which current and planned activities receive necessary resources and, just as importantly, which do not. Because district resources are usually quite constrained, freeing up the resources necessary to fully invest in activities that are crucial to and coherent with the strategy usually means cutting off the flow to others.

STAKEHOLDER RELATIONSHIPS

Stakeholders are people and groups inside and outside the organization who have a legitimate interest in the schools and can influence the success of the district's strategy. These include teachers unions, parents, students, school boards, community and advocacy groups, and local politicians and policymakers. Conducting and managing stakeholder relationships in a way that is coherent with the strategy is especially challenging because stakeholders often disagree about what success looks like or how to achieve it. However, effective strategies are informed by the views and priorities of such groups. In moving ahead, district leaders must either persuade a majority of stakeholder groups about the wisdom of their strategy or build a sufficient alliance among some that will prevent the others from becoming a disruptive force.

ENVIRONMENT

A school district's environment includes all of the external factors that can have an impact on strategy, operations, and performance. The environment in which public school districts operate is especially complex and dynamic, including the various funding sources available (both public and private); the political and policy contexts at the city, state, and national levels; the collective bargaining arrangements that are in place; and the characteristics of the particular community.

While district leaders have little direct control over the environment, they must spend significant time trying to manage its effects in order to consistently implement a districtwide strategy. The environment can affect a school system by enforcing nonnegotiable demands, constraining decision making, reducing resources, evaluating performance, and imposing sanctions. However, the environment can also serve as an enabler if district leaders can promote an understanding of the schools' needs and thus influence the regulatory and statutory, contractual, financial, and political forces that surround them.

PART IV

Large-Scale Reform

Michael Fullan

en Levin (former Deputy Minister of Education in Ontario) and I teamed up to describe the Ontario strategy in the first article in this section. Think of this as the joint effort of an insider (Ben) and an outsider (me) change agent coming together in an applied strategic direction.

The other article in this section comes from Michael Barber. Starting as the architect of Tony Blair's first reform, and now active around the world, including the United States, in advising governments on system reform, Barber is hard hitting and demanding as he urges systems to move from awful to adequate to good to great. Only the latter will save public school systems, and Barber identifies what systems need to achieve greatness in their performance.

We can expect to see more radical experiments on the part of states and governments as they push for more successful large-scale reform. The two articles in this section provide early examples of this new direction.

CHAPTER THIRTEEN

Learning About System Renewal

Ben Levin

Michael Fullan

INTRODUCTION

The introduction of the Education Reform Act (ERA) in 1988 in England was a watershed event, not just in that country but internationally. The education policies introduced by the government of Margaret Thatcher constituted a particularly large and dramatic instance of a particular approach to educational change based primarily on a belief in competition and information as the primary drivers of improvement. In essence, the changes made in the United Kingdom in and around 1988 had the following logic:

- The belief that competition in the economy as a whole drives efficiency and improvement could be applied to schools as well, so that competition among schools would lead to better outcomes for students.
- In order for schools to compete, individual schools would require much more autonomy.
- Parents would need to be able to choose the schools their children attended.

- In order to choose, parents and the public would require comparable measures of student achievement and education quality for all schools, based on a single national curriculum.

The English reforms involved much more than these four elements, and, like all large reform programs, embodied a certain number of inconsistencies (e.g. Lawton, 1994), but these points describe the essential logic on which the Thatcher government's education policy was based for a decade or more.

England was not the first country to move in this direction. New Zealand had taken some of the same steps a year or two earlier, though not as comprehensively (Levin, 2001). Some states and districts in the United States had also introduced various forms of school choice and common quality information. But from the outset, the English approach was widely seen as stronger, bigger, bolder, and as providing an important test of the validity of the basic logic of competition as the driver of improvement (Whitty, Power, & Halpin, 1998). The Blair government, especially in its first term (1997–2001), built considerably on the ERA, in particular by prioritizing literacy and numeracy and by establishing more precise accountability and capacity building components (Barber, 2007).

In the 20 years since then, many countries have moved in similar directions, though with highly variable degrees of boldness and commitment. Several states in Australia adopted forms of choice and competition. The United States, because of its size and decentralized governance structure, has seen an enormous range of reforms, many of which embody ideas of competition among schools. The current national U.S. reform program, No Child Left Behind, is based on the idea that information and competition can drive improvement although its choice components are somewhat muted.

It would, however, be a mistake to think that the world as a whole has widely emulated the ideas behind the UK reforms. For one thing, much of the world is still struggling to provide basic elementary and secondary education to all students and so is nowhere near the situation of being able to contemplate competition (which, after all, requires excess capacity). Even in the industrialized world, few European countries adopted the competitive model at more than a superficial level (Glatter, Woods, & Bagley, 1997). In Europe the results of the Program for International Student Assessment (PISA) (Organization for Economic Cooperation and Development

[OECD], 2004) have had more impact on policy than have examples from the United States or United Kingdom. While New Zealand piloted massive decentralization and choice, it did not adopt the remainder of the UK program. Several Australian states did attempt their own versions of competition, but changes in state governments often meant these reforms did not last. Canadian provinces have introduced only very modest forms of school choice. Japan and Korea, among many other countries, already had highly competitive secondary school systems, but based on examination success rather than student choice. So if one looks at the education policy world in 2007, choice and competition play a larger role than they did 20 years ago, but they are not the hegemonic model on which most public education is based, and even where they do exist they are often quite tempered.

At the same time, there have been growing concerns about basing an education strategy on choice and competition (Fuller, Elmore, & Orfield, 1996; Thrupp, 1999). PISA does give some support to decentralization, but also draws attention to the potential negative effects of increased social segregation among schools. Recent reforms in many countries attempt to address both excellence and equity through strategies that focus on improving the whole system by *raising the bar and closing the gap* for all. The OECD has in recent years given considerable attention to strategies for improving equity at all levels of the education system (OECD, 2007). These strategies attempt to combine high support and high challenge in raising the capacity at all levels of the system to engage in and pursue continuous improvement. The general policy language is moving away from seeing excellence and equity as trade-offs, towards seeing them as complementary and recognizing that a number of countries are able to achieve both.

Our focus in this article is on the lessons learned about effective change from international experience with large-scale reform over the last 20 years—and indeed, starting well before 1988. We do not attempt a full evaluation of the ERA. Instead we treat the ERA as a starting point for some impressive learning about how to bring about real and lasting improvement in student outcomes. We believe that the central lesson of large-scale educational change is this: Large-scale, sustained improvement in student outcomes requires a sustained effort to change school and classroom practices, not just structures such as governance and accountability. The heart of improvement lies in changing teaching and learning practices in thousands and thousands of classrooms, and this requires focused and sustained effort by all parts of the education system and its partners.

Our basis for making this assertion rests on a combination of our own experience and a careful reading of a wide range of research. We have read much of the literature on large-scale change and, in the case of Fullan, contributed substantially to it. Our review draws on both published and unpublished literature (cited much more extensively in Fullan, 2007) from many countries, including but not limited to the substantial literature in the United Kingdom and the United States as well as Levin's (2001) comparative study. Between us, we have been actively involved in education policy or worked closely with leaders in about 20 countries, including most English-speaking countries. We have also been involved with international policy through organizations such as the OECD and the Open Society Institute. Our discussion of high-potential strategies for large-scale reform draws heavily on our work evaluating the National Literacy and Numeracy Strategies in England from 1998 to 2002 (Earl, Watson, Levin, Leithwood, Fullan, & Torrance, 2003; Stannard & Huxford, 2007) and on the reforms in Ontario from 2003 to the present (Levin, in press).

While we make a series of general assertions in this paper, we also recognize that generalizations across countries have to be both made and regarded with caution. As already noted, in our view, national and subnational policies are shaped more by local circumstances than by common ideas (Levin, 1998). Although we outline ideas on knowledge about large-scale change in education that we think have broad applicability, their application will look different in each setting and at different points in time. That is as it should be.

Knowledge About Large-Scale Change and Renewal

Creating change in education is easy. Many governments have done it by changing funding or policies or information or governance structures. However, these changes are not necessarily improvements. There are plenty of examples of large-scale change efforts that have not produced the desired results (e.g. the discussion of a number of cities in the United States in Cuban & Usdan, 2003). Our interest is in change strategies that have the potential to create lasting improvement in a broad range of student outcomes. This is clearly not easy to do, but there are now enough examples with some success that some useful approaches are emerging. We believe that a considerable amount has been learned over the last 10 years about how to create meaningful and sustainable improvement. More to the point, we see evidence that governments are turning away from some of the simplistic approaches used earlier to embrace the kinds of principles described in this article.

For regional or national governments, our understanding of the evidence is that any education reform that is intended to be sustainable and to result in better outcomes for learners must embody something like the following seven areas of attention. Given limitations of space, we treat these here very briefly. True to the theory of action itself, it should be noted that these ideas have been "discovered" via reflective action over the past decade and more. They are interactive and mutually reinforcing: One could easily reframe the same ideas somewhat differently, resulting in a longer or shorter list. Our seven premises are

1. A small number of ambitious yet achievable goals, publicly stated

2. A positive stance with a focus on motivation

3. Multilevel engagement with strong leadership and a "guiding coalition"

4. Emphasis on capacity building with a focus on results

5. Keeping a focus on key strategies while also managing other interests and issues

6. Effective use of resources

7. Constant and growing transparency, including public and stakeholder communication and feedback

Public Goals and Targets

Schools are expected to be all things to all people. But improvement in a complex organization or system requires unrelenting focus on a few things at a time. To engender public interest and to create system focus, governments need to identify a small number (2–4) of key goals and set specific targets for improvement. Trying to improve everything all at the same time inevitably leads to dispersion of effort, burnout, and failure to achieve anything worthwhile. This means starting with those goals that are most salient in the public mind—typically things like elementary school literacy or high school graduation or student safety. Later, we discuss the need to ensure a balance between a focus on key goals and some attention to other important and often complementary issues. The small number of goals selected must be fundamental to success in other areas. Literacy, for example, is a gateway to high performance in all other domains of motivation and learning.

Goals must be public, and they must be quantifiable. Concerns about the potential distorting impact of public targets have some merit. However, in an age of political cynicism, the future of public education requires clear evidence that results are improving, and this evidence must be in a form that is readily communicated and understood to people whose knowledge of the subtleties of education is limited. Without such evidence, people will not send either their children or their money to the public schools. It is important to ensure that a few key targets do not become the sole focus of attention for the system. Careful attention to the effective and transparent use of data is important to avoid the inevitable tendency to distort numbers for other purposes (Stone, 2001). But the limitations of public attention are such that any substantial degree of complexity in the public expression of goals will lead to people losing interest in the subject.

A Positive Stance

Many government efforts to improve education have started with negative messages about schools: that they are not doing well and need strong action to improve, and even more, that educators cannot be trusted to do the job. Whether intended or not, the ERA was certainly seen that way by many educators. Yet, improvement is only possible if people are motivated, individually and collectively, to put in the effort necessary to get results. Changing practices across many, many schools will only happen when teachers, principals, and support staff see the need and commit to making the effort to improve their daily practice (Danielson & Hochschild, 1998). A central problem with many education reform strategies has been their demotivating effect on educators, who felt attacked from the outset. Our reading of the relevant evidence, not just from education but more generally, is that reform strategies must be explained and implemented in a way that engages the idealism and professional commitments of educators (Levin, 2001; Fullan, 2006). Every element of reform must keep in mind the importance of engaging educators in serious improvement.

An important challenge is to recognize that improved motivation cannot be achieved in the short run. In fact, the beginning of all eventual successes is unavoidably bumpy. However, if a reform strategy does not gain on the motivation question over time (end of year one, year two, etc.), it will fail. Building morale and motivation is also multifaceted. Appealing to educators' sense of moral purpose—their belief that education is about success for all students—is a great potential motivator but not enough by itself. That is why large-scale reform must also pay attention to other key aspects of motivation—capacity, resources, peer and leadership support and identity, and so on. It is the combination that makes the motivational difference. However, the key point to keep in mind is that any strategy that starts with attacks on the existing system is highly unlikely to produce lasting positive results, just as teachers do not succeed with students by endlessly pointing out their inadequacies. Put differently, the interactive force of the other six elements creates forms of pressure that are much more likely to motivate and reward people for taking action relative to key improvement goals.

Multilevel Engagement and Strong Leadership

Real reform requires sustained attention from many people at all levels of the education system. It is not enough for a state or national government to be fully committed, difficult as this is in itself. Many if not most schools, and, where they exist, districts or regional authorities, must also share the goals and purposes of reform and improvement. It is even better when the efforts of the school system are understood and supported by external groups such as community agencies, as this is important to the political legitimacy of the education system. There can be—indeed, there should be—room for a variety of strategies to achieve the goals, but there cannot be substantial dissent on the main purposes themselves. We call this idea *permeable connectivity*—a bit of a mouthful that basically means pursuing strategies that promote mutual interaction and influence within and across the three levels. If enough leaders across the same system engage in permeable connectivity, they change the system itself (Fullan, 2005, 2007).

Barber (2007) has articulated the idea of the "guiding coalition" around reform, that key leaders at various levels, both politicians and administrators, all understand and articulate the strategy in very similar ways, so that leadership at all levels is mutually reinforcing. As will be discussed a little later, building this kind of common understanding requires extensive and effective two-way communication.

Strong leadership does not just emerge; it must be developed and cultivated. The challenges to and potential of effective leadership development have been described by Leithwood and Levin (in press). Leadership recruitment and development must be a key part of any successful improvement strategy. Nor should leadership be confined to those in official positions. For example, reform programs should pay careful attention to building teacher leadership at the school level and to supporting effective leadership in stakeholder organizations such as teacher and other unions and parent groups, as these partners are also vital to sustainable change. Where local authorities exist, their leadership and its development, both political and managerial, is also vital to prevent bickering and finger-pointing, that is not only distracting but hurts public confidence and support.

Shared vision and ownership are the outcomes of a quality process rather than a precondition. This is important to know because it causes one to act differently in order to create ownership. Behavior often changes before beliefs. So, everything must be driven by a bias for action and learning rather than a traditional approach to endless planning before acting. Some planning is certainly necessary, but the size and prettiness of the planning document is inversely related to the amount and quality of action, and in turn to the impact on student learning (Reeves, 2006). Pfeffer and Sutton (2000) also emphasize this theme when they talk about planning as a substitute for action. The goal of leadership is to proliferate the engagement and partnership necessary for sustainable reform.

Capacity Building

Although every successful strategy must have multiple elements, the most important single item on our list is *capacity building with a focus on results*. Some 20 years ago, Fullan coined the phrase that both *pressure and support* are required for large-scale reform. This was on the right track but not precise enough. For one thing, many policymakers overdosed on the side of pressure, with the negative impacts on motivation already noted. Moreover, identifying what was wrong did not provide the next step: What do you do about it? Even when support was provided, it was segmented from pressure and was not specific enough to have an impact. Now, the integrated phrase of "capacity building with a focus on results" captures both aspects well. The focus is on results-based improvement, but "capacity to get there" is the driving priority.

Capacity building is defined as any strategy that increases the collective effectiveness of a group to raise the bar and close the gap of student learning. For us, it involves helping to develop individual and collective (1) knowledge and competencies, (2) resources, and (3) motivation. These capacities are specifically about getting results (raise the bar, close the gap). Our theory of action says that nothing lasting will happen unless people develop new capacities. At the same time, new capacities build motivation because they generate clarity, skills, and success (Stannard & Huxford, 2007).

Most change efforts are weak on capacity building, and that is one of the key reasons why they fall short. As Elmore (2004) advised, no external accountability scheme can be successful in the absence of internal accountability—the latter is none other than capacity building with a focus on results. A key part of the focus on results is what we call the *evolution of positive pressure*. An emphasis on accountability by itself produces negative pressure: pressure that does not motivate and that does not get to capacity building. Positive pressure is pressure that does motivate, that is palpably fair and reasonable and is accompanied by resources for capacity building. The more one invests in capacity building, the more one has the right to expect greater performance. The more one focuses on results fairly—comparing similar schools, using data over multiple years, providing targeted support for improvement— the more motivational leverage can be used. In our change theory, it is capacity building first, judgment second, because that is what is most motivational.

Capacity building is not a one-way transmission of knowledge. Improvement requires many opportunities for "learning in context." In fact, creating cultures where learning in context is endemic is the point. Elmore (2004, p. 73) has pinpointed the issue: "Improvement is more a function of *learning to do the right things in the settings where you work.*" He goes on to say,

The problem [is that] there is almost no opportunity for teachers to engage in continuous and sustained learning about their practice in the settings in which they actually work, observing and being observed by their colleagues in their own classrooms and classrooms of other teachers in other schools confronting similar problems. (p. 11)

Elmore then puts forward the positive implication (it is no accident that he uses the exact phrase *theory of action*):

The theory of action behind [this process of examining practice] might be stated as follows: The development of systematic knowledge about, and related to, large-scale instructional improvement requires a change in the prevailing culture of administration and teaching in schools. Cultures do not change by mandate; they change by the specific displacement of existing norms, structures, and processes by others; the process of cultural change depends fundamentally on modeling the new values and behavior that you expect to displace the existing ones. (p. 11)

In this way, learning in context actually changes the very context itself (Spillane, 2006). Contexts do improve, and this is true not only in schools but in the larger context as well. Sustainable improvement requires *lateral capacity building* in which schools and districts learn from each other. When this happens, two change forces are unleashed, namely, knowledge (best ideas flow), and motivation (people identify with larger parts of the system). For example, when principals interact across schools and even districts in this way, they become almost as concerned about the success of other schools in their network as their own school. This is an example of changing for the better the larger context within which they work.

Capacity building may require new kinds of organizational structures. One of the key features of the National Literacy and

Numeracy Strategies in England that set them apart from many other reform efforts, including most of the ERA strategies, was the creation of special-purpose organization structures to support capacity building (Earl et al., 2003). Often, the existing bureaucratic structures at various levels of the system will not be sufficient to implement and support real improvement because they are too focused on their ongoing maintenance or policy work, while capacity building requires different skills and often different people. An improvement strategy therefore also requires thought about the kinds of structures that may be needed to support the agenda.

Capacity building is not an end in itself. It needs to be linked explicitly to results. Whatever the domain, a results-oriented strategy enables and requires all levels of the system to use ongoing data as both an improvement strategy and for accountability. Schools, districts, and governments should focus on (1) how well they are progressing (comparing themselves with their own starting points), (2) how well they are doing compared to other similar groups (comparing apples to apples), and (3) how well they are doing relative to an absolute standard (e.g., 100% success).

Keeping a Focus on Key Strategies While Also Managing Other Interests and Issues

All management texts reinforce the importance of having a clear strategy and sticking with it. However, that is much harder to do in the public sector because there can be sudden leadership changes (as a result of elections, etc.), and, even more common, sudden changes in what is on the public mind due to unexpected events or media attention (Levin, 2005). When public attention shifts, so must the attention of senior government leaders. It is extraordinarily difficult to keep real, focused attention on the same set of priorities over a three- or four-year time frame.

It is also the case that in a complex public institution, such as education, there are always many competing interests at work. Various stakeholder groups have their own favorite causes as well as their own interests and will continue to advance these no matter what the official priorities may be. Many things in the system favor the status quo by diverting energy to maintenance activities at the expense of devoting resources and attention to continuous improvement. Examples include collective bargaining issues, administrative procedures, and short-term political pressures on minor issues. In a political world, these pressures cannot be ignored, but they also cannot be allowed to put the central focus at risk. As one pursues the core strategy, there must be an explicit attention to the many "distractors" that inevitably arise.

Thus, a central challenge in managing education reform is to pay sufficient attention to all the competing agendas and interests while never losing sight of or focus on the few key priorities for improvement. This is indeed a fine art. It requires strong partnerships between political leaders and their senior officials, as well as strong political leadership. It also requires, as discussed below, continuous attention to public communication to build understanding of and support for the central agenda. Staying the course relative to the small number of key priorities is crucial.

Constant Transparency Including Public and Stakeholder Communication and Feedback

Reformers often have a tendency to think that their approach is self-evident to every reasonable person. But, as discussed above, there will always be different points of view, different priorities, and different understandings in a public system. People will inevitably misunderstand or misinterpret what is happening, either from lack of understanding or for purposes of their own interests. The nature of human interaction requires constant efforts to communicate, and never more so than when some significant change from the status quo is being attempted.

Effective communication is not spin or propaganda. It is not intended to convince people of something—a feat that is in any case increasingly difficult to do given the multichannel universe and an increasingly better educated and more skeptical population. Many governments have learned that ads intended to boast of their accomplishments may hurt more than help. What is needed is frequent, honest, two-way communication about successes and challenges, about what is being attempted and its challenges and setbacks as well as accomplishments.

Communication has to address the public. Educators often forget that most voters do not have children in school or direct links to schools and tend to get their information from other people or from the media. That is why public targets and progress reporting are so important. It may be necessary to involve third-party reporting in order to provide some guarantee that public reporting is indeed accurate. Part of the challenge, discussed earlier, of ensuring that a few key targets do not distort the entire system is to have multiple forms of reporting and to provide information on many outcomes, not just those that have been chosen as the key deliverables.

Internal communication is also vital. It is amazing how many organizations put a plan in place and neglect to tell their employees what it is or to solicit staff input to it. Many teachers, we have found, are entirely unaware of their district's or state's priorities and strategies. Communication to support staff, parents, and students is equally important. Students in particular are a largely neglected potential source of support for meaningful improvement in teaching and learning practices (Fullan, 2007; Levin & Pekrul, 2007).

Any communications professional will emphasize the three secrets of effective communication—repetition, repetition, and repetition. Governments are often criticized for spending money on communications, yet good communications, as described here, must be a key part of any program of school improvement.

Finally, when communication is linked with transparent results, there is much more feedback on the validity of results, enabling celebration where there is success and critical feedback for further improvement.

Effective Use of Resources

Our reading of the evidence and experience is that some level of additional resources is essential to successful improvement, but that money is not the critical driver, and that it is just as important to pursue more effective use of existing resources. New money is important in three ways. First, it serves as a tangible sign of commitment to change for people within the system and is a critical element in building motivation for improvement. Second, it is one way of managing distractors. Collective bargaining and teachers' wages must be handled effectively to keep good people entering and staying in the profession and to prevent wage and benefit issues from turning into major problems and distractions. Third, small amounts of resources can be used to lever significant amounts of change through supporting new ways of working. For example, better professional development, or leadership development, or in-school coaching of teaching practice can all be supported with very modest increments of resources.

It is equally important to ensure that existing resources are well used. Many educational organizations do not give careful attention to the way they allocate resources and match them to priorities (Levin & Naylor, in press). Improvement of governance and leadership should be directed in part to helping leaders make more informed decisions about how to allocate staff and other resources in light of our knowledge about effective strategies to improve learning. For example, the allocation of support staff is often not linked to teaching and learning but to special education procedures. Another example would be moving administrators too frequently from school to school (Hargreaves & Fink, 2006) or failing to ensure that high-need schools received their fair share of the most skilled teachers.

CONCLUSION—BEYOND THE ERA

England has been a forerunner in large-scale reform. The 1988 legislation stimulated and informed some reforms in other countries. The reforms in England were also important in stimulating the creation of a much broader international network of scholars studying education change outside the United States. Whole new organizations, such as International Congress on School Effectiveness and Improvement (ICSEI) were given impetus by the scale and ambition of the changes in the United Kingdom. The result has been a broader program of research and intellectual discussion of large-scale reform, one that is more attentive to the importance of local context, history, and culture (Levin, 2001).

Although the ERA set a new tone in education reform, gains in student outcomes in England were more evident after the adoption of these strategies than they were from the original ERA reforms (Stannard & Huxford, 2007). The assumption in the ERA on choice and competition as the drivers of improvement has not been demonstrated to work. Jurisdictions that have relied primarily on this strategy—not just England but also in the United States, Australia, parts of Canada, and other places—have not been able to demonstrate significant gains in student outcomes. PISA (OECD, 2004) has had a powerful impact in demonstrating that countries with high success tended to have less differentiated school systems.

The result has been a much broader embrace in education policy of approaches using some or all of the elements described in this paper. Finland, the highest-scoring country in two rounds of PISA, gives little attention to competition. Singapore, another high-scoring country in international assessments, has placed considerable emphasis on leadership development and on professional learning for teachers to improve pedagogical skills. Professional networks of teachers and/or principals have been created in several places to strengthen learning across contexts. The Province of Ontario has a well-developed Literacy and Numeracy Strategy that is showing good results using much of what we describe here (Campbell & Fullan, 2006; Fullan, 2007). Recent Australian and New Zealand policy documents on literacy give primary attention to improving teachers' skills and involving parents rather than to assessment, accountability, and competition (e.g. Literacy Taskforce, 1999; Ainley & Fleming, 2000; New South Wales, 2007). However, there are still many places that are relying on top-down, policy-driven approaches to change that cannot, in our view, deliver real and lasting improvement in students' learning.

Although we believe use of change knowledge is increasing internationally, future prospects remain mixed. The inhibiting factors are threefold. First, the use of change knowledge does not represent a quick fix or the satisfying of an ideological agenda, which is what political pressures such as those giving rise to the ERA often require. Governments are almost always under more pressure to "do something" than they are to show that their policies of a few years ago are successful. Second, not only is this more complex approach to reform difficult to grasp, but it must be shared by many leaders simultaneously (the guiding coalition) for its use to spread and be consistent. This is a tall order given the turnover in leaders and the many competing pressures facing any government or school system. Third, lasting improvement does require deep cultural change in school systems, which many people resist, tacitly or otherwise. It requires hard, patient, unrelenting effort over a period of years.

On the positive side, there are three things working on behalf of the increased use of change knowledge. First, after 50 years of trying everything else, the results have not been satisfactory. The ERA certainly changed education in England, but it did not bring the improved results that had been hoped for. More and more policy makers and the public know that what has been done does not work.

This makes people more receptive to clear, promising alternative strategies.

Second, change knowledge and its specific strategic manifestations are indeed becoming more and more clear, thanks in part to an extensive international network of researchers. How it works and why it works are more evident. Ideas around capacity building are becoming the conventional wisdom, as embodied in government policy documents (such as those cited earlier) and in the work of the OECD (2007). As more jurisdictions experiment with capacity-building approaches, we learn more about how to make these work, although there is still much to learn. And while not a quick fix, it is also not open ended. We are now able to claim that using this knowledge can produce significant results within one election period—three to four years—as has been the case in Ontario (Levin, in press).

Third, we now have more leaders who are actively using and refining the knowledge—system thinkers in action (Fullan, 2005, 2007). Change knowledge then shifts from a disembodied set of facts to a deeply applied phenomenon in the minds and actions of people. Moreover, for this knowledge to have an impact, it must be actively *shared* by many people engaged in using the knowledge. We have already given some examples of such shared use in evidence, and if it continues to spread, we may have the breakthrough required for change knowledge to have an enduring place in the field of education reform. Large-scale, successful reform occurs in a thousand small ways during the journey.

The next phase of large-scale education improvement will involve more emphasis on strategies that affect all classrooms, and a focus on key elements that foster ongoing quality, as well as a link to other core elements essential for societal reform. Reforms primarily focused on structure and governance, such as the ERA, are now and will continue to be, we think, less dominant. The last 20 years have taught us that changing structures does not yield better results for students, and at the same time we have learned more about how to change teaching and learning practices on a large scale. On classroom instructional change, Fullan, Hill, and Crévola (2006) describe a model for getting inside all classrooms where each and every teacher is learning all the time. Countries will pay more explicit policy attention to the quality of the teaching force (OECD, 2005) and of school principals and leaders at other levels, while also recognizing the importance of professional motivation through public respect for educators coupled with positive pressure. Other core elements that will be part of a more comprehensive approach to "capacity building with a focus on results" will include deep attention (finally) to early-childhood capacity building from conception to age five, well being of students of all ages, and adult education particularly as a complement to the development of young children.

Most of the OECD countries have done an impressive job of providing a solid education and improving the life chances of 50% to 60% of the population. The ERA in England was one of the seismic events that set both policy and research looking for a higher bar. But the ERA strategies were insufficient to produce the necessary improvements. Growing evidence outlined in this paper indicates that this new level of success requires a different strategy, one that tackles success for all students through changes in practice in all schools as well as the related policy changes. We believe that there has been a quantum shift in the past decade in recognizing what will be needed to achieve this most ambitious goal.

REFERENCES

Ainley, J., & Fleming, M. (2000). *Learning to read in the early primary years*. East Melbourne, Victoria, Australia: Catholic Education Commission of Victoria.

Barber, M. (2007). *Instruction to deliver*. London: Politico, Methuen.

Campbell, C., & Fullan, M. (2006). *Unlocking the potential for district-wide reform*. Unpublished report. Toronto, Ontario, Canada: Ontario Ministry of Education. Retrieved from http://www.michaelfullan.ca/Articles_06/Articles_06a.htm

Cuban, L., & Usdan, M., (Eds.). (2003). *Powerful reforms with shallow roots: Improving America's urban schools*. New York: Teachers College Press.

Danielson, M., & Hochschild, J. (1998). Changing urban education: Lessons, cautions, prospects, in C. Stone (Ed.), *Changing urban education* (pp. 277–295). Lawrence, KS: University Press of Kansas.

Earl, L., Watson, N., Levin, B., Leithwood, K., Fullan, M., & Torrance, N. (2003). *Watching and learning 3: Final report of the OISE/UT evaluation of the implementation of the national literacy and numeracy strategies*. Prepared for the Department for Education and Skills, England. Toronto, Ontario, Canada: OISE/University of Toronto. Retrieved from http://www.standards.dfes.gov.uk/literacy/publications

Elmore, R. F. (2004). *School reform from the inside out.* Cambridge, MA: Harvard University Press.

Fullan, M. (2005). *Leadership and sustainability.* Thousand Oaks, CA: Corwin.

Fullan, M. (2006). *Turnaround leadership.* San Francisco: Jossey-Bass.

Fullan, M. (2007). *The new meaning of educational change* (4th ed.). New York: Teachers College Press.

Fullan, M., Hill, P., & Crévola, C. (2006). *Breakthrough.* Thousand Oaks, CA: Corwin.

Fuller, B., Elmore, R. F., & Orfield, G. (Eds.). (1996). *Who chooses, who loses?* New York: Teachers College Press.

Glatter, R., Woods, P., & Bagley, C. (Eds.). (1997). *Choice and diversity in schooling: Perspectives and prospects.* London: Routledge.

Hargreaves, A., & Fink, D. (2006). *Sustainable leadership.* San Francisco: Jossey-Bass.

Lawton, D. (1994). *The Tory mind on education 1979–1994.* London: Falmer Press.

Leithwood, K., & Levin, B. (in press). Understanding and assessing the impact of leadership development. In J. Lumby & N. Foskett (Eds.), *International handbook on the preparation and development of school leaders.* Mahwah, NJ: Lawrence Erlbaum.

Levin, B. (in press). Sustainable, large-scale education renewal. *Journal of Educational Change.*

Levin, B. (1998). An epidemic of education policy: (What) can we learn from each other? *Comparative Education 34*(2), 131–141.

Levin, B. (2001). *Reforming education: From origins to outcomes.* London: RoutledgeFalmer.

Levin, B. (2005). *Governing education.* Toronto, Ontario, Canada: University of Toronto Press.

Levin, B., & Naylor, N. (in press). Using resources effectively in education. In J. Burger, P. Klinck, & C. Webber (Eds.), *A General theory of everything in education.* Dordrecht, the Netherlands: Kluwer.

Levin, B., & Pekrul, S. (2007). Building student voice for school improvement. In A. Cook-Sather & D. Thiessen (Eds.), *International handbook of student experience* (pp. 711–726). Dordrecht, the Netherlands: Springer.

Literacy Taskforce. (1999). *Report of the Literacy Task Force.* Wellington: Government of New Zealand.

New South Wales. (2007). *Literacy and numeracy action plan.* Government of New South Wales.

OECD. (2004). *Learning for tomorrow's world: First results from PISA 2003.* Paris: OECD.

OECD. (2005). *Attracting, developing and retaining effective teachers—final report: Teachers matter.* Paris: OECD.

OECD. (2007). *Fair and inclusive education: Report of the thematic review on equity in lifelong learning.* Unpublished draft report. Paris: OECD.

Pfeffer, J., & Sutton, R. (2000). *The knowing-doing gap.* Boston: Harvard Business School.

Reeves, D. (2006). *The learning leader.* Alexandria, VA: Association for Supervision and Curriculum Development.

Spillane, J. (2006). *Distributed leadership.* San Francisco: Jossey-Bass.

Stannard, J., & Huxford, L. (2007). *The literacy game.* London: Routledge.

Stone, D. (2001). *Policy paradox.* New York: Norton.

Thrupp, M. (1999). *Schools making a difference: Let's be realistic.* Buckingham, UK: Open University Press.

Whitty, G., Power, S., & Halpin, D. (1998). *Devolution and choice in education.* Buckingham, UK: Open University Press.

Send correspondence to

Ben Levin, Ontario Institute for Studies in Education, University of Toronto, Canada. E-mail: blevin@oise.utoronto.ca

CHAPTER FOURTEEN

Education, Equity, and the Economy

Michael Barber

INTRODUCTION

This article brings three distinct perspectives to bear. First, as an outsider with some knowledge of education systems around the world, I want to comment on how the school system in the United States looks against international benchmarks.

Second, as a battle-hardened veteran of the Blair government's controversial school reforms, I want to draw some lessons from that broadly successful but also messy, error-strewn experience, which took England from below average to above average in international benchmarks, but not yet world-class.

Third, I want to comment on the struggle, over more than two centuries, to close the gap between the American dream and the American reality.

This article is an amended version of a keynote speech "Neither Rest Nor Tranquility" at the National Education Summit in Washington DC on September 15, 2008, and it was originally published by WestEd in 2009 as a Policy Perspectives paper, *Neither Rest Nor Tranquility: Education and the American Dream in the 21st Century.*

I believe school reform in the United States is at a critical juncture. In the next year or so it will be necessary to choose between two broad options: on the one hand, a retreat to the comfortable, introverted, input-focused, evidence-light approach that characterized education reform in the last three decades of the 20th century, during which time Americans tried and failed to live up to the towering ambitions of the civil rights movement; on the other, an advance to the demanding, outward-looking, results-focused, evidence-informed approach towards which some promising progress has recently been made.

That choice will have to be made in governors' mansions, state capitols, city halls, and school boards across the country, but symbolically and substantively the reauthorization of the No Child Left Behind Act—the most important piece of education legislation for many years and the most equitable legislation of the new century so far—will be the moment of truth.

The decisive factors in the making of this choice will be the accumulating evidence of what works (and what doesn't) and the courage of those who lead public education and who shape opinion within the system and among businesses and communities. To paraphrase Robert Frost, two roads are diverging in a wood and the choice this country makes—you make—will make all the difference.

As you prepare to face that fateful choice, I want today to do three things—glance back at the past, assess the present, and sketch the future.

SECTION 1: THE PAST

In 1955, the year General Motors achieved a U.S. market share of 50% (Loomis, 2006) and two years before the launch of Sputnik undermined America's post-war confidence, the American high school reached its zenith—at least for white kids. A year earlier, the Supreme Court had momentously decided that the education those white kids received should ultimately be available to all, setting the terms of debate for the ensuing decades.

Up to that time—and indeed beyond—the United States had a huge comparative advantage over all other countries in the provision of universal, general education as Claudia Goldin and Larry Katz (2008) have recently demonstrated. "During the first three quarters of the [20th] century educational attainment rose rapidly" (p. 3), they argue.

This was largely due to the existence of universally available high school education but also to the growing availability of college. Because good schooling brings very long-run benefits, America's educational leadership over the rest of the world brought substantial relative gains in economic growth right through to the end of the 20th century. Even now, the United States leads the world in the college graduate share of those aged 55 to 64 years.

But in the last quarter of the 20th century, educational attainment in the United States stagnated. Countries that, educationally-speaking, had been trailing in America's wake for most of the 20th century began to catch up. As Goldin and Katz explain,

> The slowdown in the educational attainment of young Americans at the end of the twentieth century is especially striking when compared with the acceleration of schooling among many nations in Europe and parts of Asia, where educational change has been exceedingly rapid. (p. 7)

This relative slide in the educational performance of the United States has had, and will continue to have, economic consequences. Since "A greater level of education results in higher labour productivity [and] . . . tends to foster a higher rate of aggregate growth" (Goldin, & Katz, 2008, p. 41), relative weakness in education puts at risk long-term growth rates. The recent work of Hanushek, Jamison, Jamison, and Woessmann (2008) reinforces the case by demonstrating the strong, positive correlation between the performance of countries in Program for International Student Achievement (PISA) and Trends in International Math and Science Study (TIMSS) and their rates of economic growth. Having looked at the international comparisons in science and math over the past 40 years, they conclude, "higher levels of cognitive skill appear to play a major role in explaining differences in economic growth." They show that the United States has fallen relatively in these international comparisons and is now at best average.

This slippage is not the result of a lack of investment, which remains relatively high in the United States. Rather, it reflects—to use hard economic terms—a lack of productivity. The point is reinforced by the fact that in international comparisons of younger children, the United States does relatively well, which, given the country's wealth, is what you would expect. The problem is that, as they get older, children make less progress each year than children in the best performing countries. Here, we're not just talking about poor kids in poor neighborhoods; we're talking about most kids in most neighborhoods.

Moreover, there is no comfort in the belief that future economic success depends not so much on the overall levels of cognitive skill in the population but rather on ensuring that at least a few brilliant rocket scientists come through. Hanushek et al. (2008) show convincingly that in the 21st century, having "a substantial cadre of high performers" and "near universal basic skills" (p. 68) are both essential. In short, the choice is a false one and the debate a distraction.

Summarizing then, long-term, the future success of the American economy will depend on significantly improving the U.S. school (and college) system with all the urgency that can be mustered. Indeed, because of the inevitable time lag, even with the most rapid imaginable education reform, it will be some years before the impact is felt on economic growth. No wonder business leaders often play a leading role in driving school reform in this country; they see the hard edge of these issues. It is one thing in the global economy to offshore unskilled jobs because labor is cheaper elsewhere; it is quite another thing to offshore highly skilled jobs simply because the qualified workforce can't be found—but too often this has become the reality.

Equally important, though, school reform in this country has never been just a question of economics, important though that is. From the beginning of the Republic, education was seen as fundamental to building democracy and extending freedom. Jefferson (1900) was giving expression to a universal belief when he said, "If a nation expects to be ignorant and free in a state of civilisation, it expects what never was and never will be" (p. 605). This idealism was one of the reasons why the United States made much earlier and more rapid progress towards universal public education than many countries in Europe.

From the 1950s onward, the realization of this ideal, an ideal which underpinned the American dream, became central to the burgeoning civil rights movement, at first in the Deep South where grotesque educational inequality was placed firmly on the agenda by the Brown versus the Board of Education decision and later in the northern cities as the hopes of the diaspora all too often turned to despair.

There were, of course, many strands to the civil rights movement, all wonderfully woven together in Taylor Branch's (1988, 1998, 2007) monumental trilogy, *America in the King Years.*

It is clear from his account that the leaders of the civil rights movement believed firmly that once equal access to school and college had been achieved, equal success would follow. Listen to King speaking to African American school students in Cleveland in 1964: "doors of opportunity are opening now that were not opened to your mothers and fathers. The great challenge facing you is to be ready to enter those doors" (Branch, 1998, p. 519). If they are ready, he implies, access will be enough.

Listen to President Johnson promising "every child a place to sit and a teacher to learn from" (Branch, 1998, p. 311)—he makes the same assumption that access would be enough. While some civil rights leaders expected it to take decades to make up the ground—Bob Moses estimated it would take "fifty years to work this through" (Branch, 1998, p. 479)—all expected that the ground would be made up in time. In relation to education, those expectations have not been realized.

Dig deeper than the headlines and the evidence is compelling. Not only does the United States perform somewhat below the Organization for Economic Cooperation and Development (OECD) averages in the recent PISA (OECD, 2007), it also suffers from a very high socioeconomic impact on student performance. In other words, rather than overcoming the social differences children bring with them when they start school, the U.S. system—like ours in the United Kingdom—tends to reinforce them. As Goldin and Katz (2008) have argued, "The slowdown in the growth of educational attainment . . . is the single most important factor increasing wage differentials since 1980 and is a major contributor to increased family inequality" (p. 3).

Those who led the civil rights movement, whether in Congress, churches, or communities, must surely be devastated by the actual outcomes 40 or 50 years later. We know now that access to school is not enough. It is success in school that matters. We know that, at the heart of education reform, at the heart of success—not just access—is the quality of what happens in classrooms—the skills and knowledge, the expectations and ambitions, the consistency and dedication that teachers bring to the task of enabling students, whatever their background, to achieve the standards necessary for life, work, and citizenship in the 21st century. Though no one believes it would be enough on its own, achieving the ambitions for 2014 set by No Child Left Behind (NCLB) would be a great start. This far-from-easy task has become, I would venture to suggest, the emerging frontier in the drive to realize civil rights in this country.

History suggests, therefore, that in the next few years there is a great challenge facing America. Both future economic success and the wider aspirations at the heart of the very idea of America depend on vastly improving the outcomes of public education. The great threat to the country's future is that for a range of reasons it might fail to rise to this challenge. Then, for many, the American dream will never be more than a dream. The great opportunity is that a combination of business and civil rights leaders, along with the cross-party consensus that passed NCLB, could become unstoppable. Right now, the issue hangs in the balance.

SECTION 2: THE PRESENT

Let me start by assessing the negative side of the ledger—my fears. One worry I have is the sheer difficulty of getting things done in this country compared to many other countries, including my own. Of course, successful large-scale change is never easy, but in the Blair era, when the government had a large majority in Parliament and significant popular support, rapid progress was possible—as of course were rapid blunders!

Then recognize the power and organization of those who defend the status quo, face up to the legacy of failed attempts to bring about bold reform, and the result is a widespread sense of defeat in people's heads before they even begin. Across the country, people sigh, along with the Russian Prime Minister in the 1990s, who said on leaving office, "We tried to do better but everything turned out as usual" (Barber, 2007, p. 72).

Moreover, these organizational and cultural barriers within the system are compounded by the worrying lack of anxiety among the American people about public education. It seems that the public is resigned to the state of their public schools rather than satisfied or delighted with them. *Education Next*'s Fall 2008 issue (Howell, West, & Peterson, 2008) finds that if parents could issue letter grades to the system, as schools do to students, just 20% would give an A or B. People are significantly more satisfied with their police forces and post offices. Even so, there is little recognition that unless public education significantly improves in the near future, there is a disaster in the making. Education systems don't fail with the suddenness of a natural disaster, but the consequences can be just as devastating. In a moment of despair, James Baldwin (1998) once observed that civilizations are destroyed not by wickedness but by spinelessness (p. 318).

Fortunately, these anxieties are balanced by very real grounds for hope. To start with, wherever I go in America, I sense growing recognition among the country's leaders at local, state, and national levels that public education needs fixing. Furthermore, many of these leaders are ready to look abroad as well as at home for solutions. The growing interest from states in the American Diploma Project is a case in point.

Moreover, not the least consequence of the No Child Left Behind Act is much greater clarity in the data about the extent of the problem. The diagnosis is becoming clearer and, while this doesn't automatically lead to the cure, it is a major step forward.

In addition—again assisted by the data—we are increasingly well informed about, to use Tony Blair's favorite phrase, what works. There are chains of schools such as the Knowledge is Power Program (KIPP), Aspire, and Green Dot that demonstrably succeed where many in the past have failed. There are whole systems such as Boston, Chicago, and New York City, which are driving bold reform and delivering results. There are organizations, such as Teach for America, the New Teacher Project, and New Leaders for New Schools, showing how apparently insurmountable human capital challenges can in fact be surmounted. There are not-for-profit organizations such as Education Trust and Achieve with deep expertise in crucial areas. We have foundations—Gates, and Broad and Dell, for example—willing to take risks and invest substantially in bold alternatives to the inadequacies of the present. At state and local levels, there are community organizations and foundations acting with a similar sense of purpose. Never before has there been so much insight into how to bring about successful change, nor such substantial capacity to deliver it. The question is whether political and educational leaders can seize that insight and capacity and bring irreversible progress.

There is a further point; the very international comparisons that make such depressing reading for the United States (and challenge the United Kingdom too), also indicate a way forward. They demonstrate what can be done—with evident progress in less than a decade—with a combination of the right strategy and courageous, sustained leadership. Singapore's story over 40 years is truly inspirational. So, in an entirely different culture, is Finland's over 30 years. Poland made remarkable progress in the last decade. The reforms in Alberta and Ontario, just across your northern border, are working too. It can be done.

Which leads to my final ground for hope—the No Child Left Behind Act itself. Here was legislation that reached across political divides and set ambitious goals. It put no ceiling on educational performance, but for the first time it fixed in legislation a high floor. It has put the achievement gap on the agenda from sea to shining sea. To set a date for delivery as soon as 2014 was aspirational certainly; some critics say it is unrealistic and the due date should be postponed, perhaps indefinitely.

Others say, provide the preschool and the capacity first, and we'll come to the accountability later. Even if the American people would accept a "pay first and ask questions later" approach, this argument fails to recognize the degree of urgency. Moreover, the fact that there are schools right now achieving those goals surely suggests significant delay would be a mistake. In any case, from the perspective of the Freedom Summer of 1964, far from looking too soon, 2014 looks half a century too late. As the then Vice President said, rejecting pleas for patience, on the 100th anniversary of the Gettysburg Address, "It is empty to plead that the solution to the dilemmas of the present rests on the hands of a clock. The solution is in our hands" (Johnson, 1963).

Across the country, there are promising, albeit early, signs that—prompted by NCLB—progress is being made. Performance is improving—not enough but at least heading in the right direction. Achievement gaps are narrowing—not yet transformatively but increments are better than nothing.

So for me, NCLB is a source of hope. The question it raises to my mind is not "Should it be reversed or abandoned?" but "How can it be refined and followed through?" In my last section I want to turn to this.

Section 3: The Future

It is clear that for all its qualities, NCLB does need refinement. It is rare for any law in the world to pass legislature without blemish and rarer still not to find ways of improving it once implementation begins. There are plenty of people much better informed than I am about the finer points of this particular piece of legislation, and the Commission on NCLB (which the Aspen Institute supported) has published a distinguished and instructive report on the subject. A number of refinements in particular stand out, from an international perspective.

First, the power of the Act depends crucially on the quality of the assessments being used. Where poor tests are used, the information they provide will be misleading, with potentially dire consequences for the students themselves when they leave school and meet the real world coming the other way. One option for solving this problem was advocated recently by *The New York Times* ("How well," 2008), and would involve asking National Assessment of Educational Progress (NAEP) to create a rigorous test to be given free to states— with those that choose not to use it being publicly identified and therefore asked to explain themselves. I'm not sure whether this is the best solution, but the direction is certainly right.

Second, the introduction of growth models has brought welcome refinement to the accountability requirements, and it makes sense to build on this development. Growth models are helpful as a measure of progress and explanation of the scale of the challenge; they are dangerous when they become a justification for poor performance or lower expectations. Our experience in England suggests growth or value-added models should be combined with a continuing focus on the absolute outcomes, which are all that matter to students when they leave school. They need to be part of a refined, modern, student-based data system, which puts the evidence at the fingertips of every professional at every level.

Third, districts and states need to develop the capacity to act decisively in response to the data. They need to be able to recognize and reward those who succeed, especially those who succeed in challenging circumstances; they also need to intervene effectively where progress is not what it needs to be. In England, not without difficulty and controversy, we did develop this latter capacity. Under pressure from us in central government, our equivalent of school districts did learn how to intervene effectively in failing schools. They did not apply prepackaged interventions in mechanical sequence; instead, they diagnosed the problem in each school and tailored the solution accordingly, answering the only question that matters in these circumstances—"What do we need to do to get these kids a good education as fast as possible?"

This raises my fourth point: Successful education reform is as much about means as it is about ends. Getting the policy right is difficult to be sure; but it is relatively easy compared to making it happen, consistently and effectively, so that the benefits are felt in every classroom. Policy failure is as often a failure of implementation as it is of concept. Systems need to develop both the technical capacity and the necessary mindset to deliver results. This is what, in the Blair administration, we self-mockingly called "deliverology," but, when we applied it systematically, it worked. An American equivalent is needed across the country to ensure the ambitions of NCLB are realized rather than eroded. As one of our more hapless kings—Charles I—once observed (shortly before they cut off his head), "There is more to the doing than bidding it be done."

Fifth, there is much more to do to ensure there is a highly effective (more important than highly qualified) teacher in every classroom and a highly effective principal in every school. It is especially important to ensure that the schools facing the toughest challenges have access, as soon as possible, to the most talented teachers and leaders. Doing so requires root-and-branch reform of inherited, traditional, bureaucratic systems of recruiting and training teachers and leaders, of paying and rewarding them and of shaping their incentives, both short-term and long-term, including pension arrangements. There needs to be a constant focus on developing talent and building capacity. At the moment, all around America, I see fine examples of what is required—Teach for America, the National Institute for School Leadership, KIPP's leadership development programs, and New York City's Leadership Academy, for example—but at the moment these remain exceptions to the rule, not the rule itself.

In relation to human capital, there is a more profound, underlying question. As McKinsey's Report, *How the World's Best Performing School Systems Come Out on Top* (Barber & Mourshed, 2007) makes clear, the world's best systems are recruiting teachers who have both the right personal qualities and come from the top third of the graduate distribution; in the United States, most teachers are from the bottom third. Without improving their underlying capacity to attract talented people, education systems will struggle to compete in future.

For the United States, the question of where in the long run it will find sufficient teachers of real quality, especially in science and math, remains unanswered. I came across a medium-sized state with great universities—I won't name it—that produced just one new physics teacher last year. Just one. Increasing the supply of talent into teaching will require, in addition to major changes in policy, a change in the way teachers are perceived. Teach for America (TFA) and similar programs are beginning to bring that about—but only beginning.

Changing a culture also requires leadership from those in government, business, and the not-for-profit sectors. The chances of success would be greatly enhanced if teacher leaders also became advocates of reform. In the early 1990s, when I worked for a teacher union in England, I suggested turning the traditional case for investment in teachers on its head. Instead of continuing to argue that if the government increased our pay we might consider improving the system, I suggested we should embrace account-ability, improve the system, and then tell the public, "Look, now you can see a system worth investing in."

Accepting this case at the time required too great a leap of faith. However, history is instructive. In spite of teacher opposition, accountability was imposed, schools did improve, and, as a result, the biggest ever increases in investment in education, including in teachers' pay and professional development, did follow. Blair called it "Investment for Reform." While teachers did not always enjoy the journey, they arrived at a much better, if more challenging, destination. Given the wide range of opportunities available, talented people won't flock into a profession with lockstep conditions and a beleaguered image. Nor will skeptical citizens continue to invest precious tax dollars in a system that doesn't seem to be working. Citizens the world over, like good businesses, prefer to invest in success.

The framework described below could be adopted as a starting point for this dialogue between government and the teaching profession.

It could provide a common language for the dialogue between government and the professions. That alone would be a major improvement on talking past each other, which has been so common in many countries including the United States. Right from the outset, government needs to foster a strong relationship with those in any

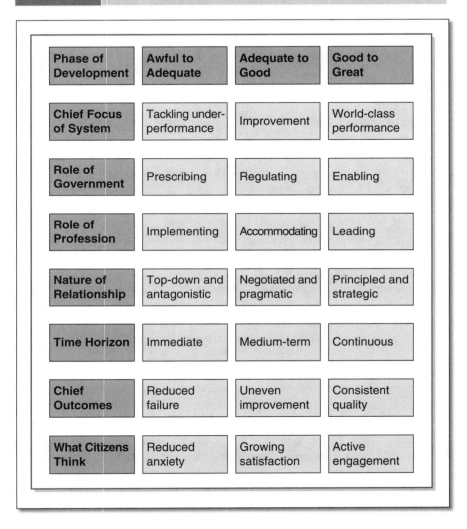

Figure 14.1   How the Relationship Between Government and Professions Could Transform Public Services

Phase of Development	Awful to Adequate	Adequate to Good	Good to Great
Chief Focus of System	Tackling under-performance	Improvement	World-class performance
Role of Government	Prescribing	Regulating	Enabling
Role of Profession	Implementing	Accommodating	Leading
Nature of Relationship	Top-down and antagonistic	Negotiated and pragmatic	Principled and strategic
Time Horizon	Immediate	Medium-term	Continuous
Chief Outcomes	Reduced failure	Uneven improvement	Consistent quality
What Citizens Think	Reduced anxiety	Growing satisfaction	Active engagement

service who are out in front. If these education leaders can express impatience with the slow pace of change, it helps to counterbalance the drag effect of those who want to slow things down. Indeed, this alliance with successful leaders is a key part of that process of building the ever-widening circles of leadership on which successful reform depends.

Certainly, it is in everyone's interest to make the attempt to create a principled relationship between government and teachers. The demand for public schools of real quality that are available to all is overwhelming; those who work in the public schools would surely prefer to be more motivated and more successful (rather than less), while governments in the next decade will find they need to sign up to this vision too if they are to succeed in meeting bold aspirations. It will require professions that embrace transparency, recognize the value of consistently high-quality and reliable processes, as well as personalization, and promote greater urgency, instead of resisting it. It will require governments to engage in constant, informed dialogue, stick to priorities, avoid gimmicks, and admit mistakes. On both sides, a nonnegotiable commitment to continuous professional learning will be essential. Delivering sustained system improvement and consistent world-class performance will be an exacting challenge for whole systems. System leaders around the world are just beginning to understand what it will take.

This raises my sixth point, because it will take serious resourcing, and at present in the United States, both the extent and distribution of funding for public schools are problematic. International benchmarks suggest that America's overall expenditure on schools is above the average, but compared to other countries, two questions of distribution stand out. The first is that, even after funding equity suits, often more money per student is spent in wealthier areas than poorer ones. It is easy to see how this came about; but to an outside observer in the early 21st century, this disparity makes no sense at all. If all young people are to reach high standards, as NCLB envisages, then the system has to provide greater support to those with furthest to go.

U.S. funding distribution is also skewed in another way, which receives less comment. A much lower proportion of it actually reaches the classroom than in the best performing systems; much more of it is tied up in administration. Of course, good administration matters, but every dollar spent on unnecessary administration is a dollar that could have assisted that welfare child reach for the stars.

In England, we required by law our "districts" to devolve the vast bulk of the funding for schools to the schools themselves. Each school now has a three year delegated budget, based on a published formula. This direction was set by the Thatcher government and continued by all its successors. In effect, the burden of proof was reversed—a pound (or dollar) should be spent at the level of the school unless there is a convincing case for spending it elsewhere. Any government in England that sought to return to the old opaque system would have a riot on its hands.

Along with the money, schools need to be given responsibility for how it is spent. The PISA evidence shows that increased management autonomy at the school level is associated with better results, but this lesson remains to be learned in many parts of this country. Recently in a northern U.S. city, I came across a good school principal setting out to turn around a failing school. She had all the right ideas but had no control over which teachers were employed at her school. She even needed permission from a teacher to visit a classroom. What chance did she have? The contrast with the nearby charter school, in similar social circumstances, was dramatic. Accountability and autonomy need to go together. The question for the United States is not just how many charter schools it wants but how soon all schools can have charter-like autonomy.

This leads to my seventh and final point. The PISA evidence indicates strongly that there are benefits in holding schools to account through standards-based external assessments. In the global economy, the question of national standards inescapably arises. The emerging bipartisan alliance in favor of common or national—as distinct from federal—standards suggests growing recognition that the United States needs them to be fewer, clearer, and higher. Moreover, *Education Next*'s recent poll (Howell et al., 2008) showed almost 70% support in the population for national standards—and over half of all public school teachers agreed.

The truth is that across the world, standards in math, science, and English will inevitably be set by global benchmarks in a globalized economy. Quite simply, to succeed countries will need world-class standards; algebra and geometry don't change at the Rio Grande or the 49th Parallel.

From this perspective, the question of national standards is straightforward; they will arrive anyway eventually. The only questions are whether they do so by accident or design, haphazardly or systematically, sooner or later. As they used to say in the civil rights decade, "If not now, when?"

CONCLUSION

The choice facing the United States is, as I began by saying, a stark one. It will shape America's capacity to succeed over the decades ahead in the profoundly challenging global economy; it will shape, too, whether the American dream in a stunningly diverse America, is genuinely open to every citizen. This is why progressive business leaders and civil rights leaders stand together. They know that the aspirations unlocked in the dawn of the civil rights movement have only partially been fulfilled. The school system has improved in many ways since that time, but surely no American can be satisfied by the outcomes. There is no ceiling on what individual Americans can achieve, but though enshrined in legislation, the high floor, on which economic success and social justice depend, has yet to be built. For those committed to a vibrant, successful America where the American Dream and the American reality more closely coincide, there can surely be, in Martin Luther King's phrase of old, "neither rest, nor tranquility" (Hansen, 2003, p. 75). It will be a long, hard road. More and more people are watching the United States, and hoping.

Counting on its success in this endeavor are not just children and families across this great country, not just the future of the American economy, not just the idea of the American dream, but all of us around the world. In the 20th century, a strong, generous, outward-looking America was a decisive factor in enabling humanity to rise and meet the challenges it faced. As Goldin and Katz (2008) have demonstrated, public education was central to making that possible. How much more important for everyone then is United States education in the 21st century, when the world is so much more complicated and the clock is ticking?

At the bottom of the staircase in No.10, just outside the Prime Minister's office, there is an exceptional photograph of Winston Churchill. Facing the camera, he glowers with such defiance that, even at that uncertain hour, wartime defeat must have seemed inconceivable to the onlooker. In fact, I'm told the real cause of his mighty frown is that the photographer had forced him to put down his cigar! Be that as it may, the time has surely come to heed his famous words, "America always does the right thing but only after it has exhausted all the alternatives." In education reform, those alternatives have indeed been exhausted. It is time for America to do the right thing.

REFERENCES

Baldwin, J. (1998). *Collected essays* (T. Morrison, Ed.). New York: Library of America.

Barber, M. (2007). *Instruction to deliver: Tony Blair, public services and the challenge of achieving targets.* London: Methuen.

Barber, M., & Mourshed, M. (2007, September). *How the world's best performing school systems come out on top.* Retrieved March 9, 2009 from http://www.closingtheachievementgap.org/cs/ctag/view/resources/111

Branch, T. (1988). *Parting the waters: America in the King years, 1954–63.* New York: Simon & Schuster.

Branch, T. (1998). *Pillar of fire: America in the King years, 1963–65.* New York: Simon & Schuster.

Branch, T. (2007). *At Canaan's edge: America in the King years, 1965–68.* New York: Simon & Schuster.

Goldin, C., & Katz, L. (2008). *The race between education and technology.* Cambridge, MA: Harvard University Press.

Hansen, D. D. (2003). *The dream: Martin Luther King, Jr., and the speech that inspired a nation.* New York: HarperCollins.

Hanushek, E., Jamison, D. T., Jamison, E. A., & Woessmann, L. (2008, Spring). Education and economic growth: It's not just going to school, but learning something while there that matters [Electronic version]. *Education Next, 8*(2), 62–70.

How well are they really doing? [Editorial]. (2008, August 12). *The New York Times,* p. A20.

Howell, W., West, M. R., & Peterson, P. E. (2008, Fall). The 2008 Education Next-PEPG survey of public opinion [Electronic version]. *Education Next, 8*(4), 13–26.

Jefferson, T. (1900). *The Jeffersonian cyclopedia* (J. P. Foley, Ed.). New York: Funk & Wagnalls Company.

Johnson, L. B. (1963, May 30). Remarks at Gettysburg on Civil Rights [Transcript]. Retrieved March 9, 2009, from http://millercenter.org/scripps/archive/speeches/detail/3380

Loomis, C. (2006, February 20). The tragedy of General Motors. *Fortune, 153*(3). Retrieved March 9, 2009, from http://money.cnn.com/magazines/fortune/fortune_archive/2006/02/20/8369111/index.htm

OECD. (2007, December). *PISA report.* Paris: Author.

Index

CORWIN

A SAGE Company

The Corwin logo—a raven striding across an open book—represents the union of courage and learning. Corwin is committed to improving education for all learners by publishing books and other professional development resources for those serving the field of PreK–12 education. By providing practical, hands-on materials, Corwin continues to carry out the promise of its motto: **"Helping Educators Do Their Work Better."**